# JONATHAN EDWARDS:
## BEYOND THE MANUSCRIPTS

Toby K. Easley

AN IMPRINT OF FEDER INK PUBLISHING
FORT WORTH, TEXAS

Copyright © 2016 Toby K. Easley

All Rights Reserved. This book may not be reproduced, in whole or in part, including illustrations, in any form (beyond that copying permitted by Sections 107 and 108 of the U.S. Copyright Law and except by reviewers for the public press), without written permission from the publishers.

COVER IMAGES: *Engraving by R Babson & J Andrews; Print by Wilson & Daniels [Public domain]*
*https://commons.wikimedia.org/wiki/File%3AJonathan_Edwards_engraving.jpg*
*Manuscript Image courtesy of Beinecke Rare Book and Manuscript Library, Yale University*

Book Design by GKS Creative, Nashville

Printed in the United States of America

First Printing, 2016

ISBN 978-0-9972179-1-9 (hardcover)

ISBN 978-0-9972179-0-2 (softcover)

*Feder Ink*
PUBLISHING

www.federinkpublishing.com

# CONTENTS

**INTRODUCTION**
Jonathan Edwards: Beyond The Manuscripts ................................. 1

**CHAPTER 1**
Jonathan Edwards's Auditory Learning and Development ................ 13

    A Father's Influence ................................................................. 16

    A Grandfather's Influence ........................................................ 17

    Contemporary Application of Stage One .................................. 18

**CHAPTER 2**
Jonathan Edwards's Development Using a Full Manuscript ............. 27

    Jonathan Edwards's First Sermon in New York City ................. 29

    Transition from New York to Bolton ....................................... 36

    Jonathan Edwards and the Bolton Ministry from
    1723 to 1724 ........................................................................... 37

    Contemporary Application of Stage Two ................................. 42

**CHAPTER 3**
Jonathan Edwards's Progression from the Manuscripts to
Outline Forms ............................................................................... 49

    The Development of Edwards's Early Preaching ...................... 52

    Northampton Preaching from 1729 Through the 1730s .......... 53

    Contemporary Application of Stage Three ............................... 56

## CHAPTER 4
Jonathan Edwards's Transitions from the Great Awakening Until 1750 .................................................................................... 63

    Northampton and the "Sinners" Sermon ................................. 66

    Edwards's Development of Sermon Notes ............................... 68

    Northampton 1742 Sermon on Hebrews 12:29 ....................... 69

    Northampton Preaching: Development Continues .................. 72

    Northampton Sermon from 1745 ............................................. 73

    Northampton's Fear of Edwards's Persuasive Preaching ............. 76

    Conclusion to the Northampton Communion Conroversy, 1750 ................................................................... 81

    The Northampton "Farewell Sermon," July 1, 1750 ................ 87

    Contemporary Application of Stage Four ................................. 93

## CHAPTER 5
Jonathan Edwards's Multifaceted Maturation and Transitional Abilities as a Missionary Preacher and a College President .............. 101

    Stockbridge and a New Homiletic .......................................... 102

    "Heaven's Dragnet": An Early Indian Sermon ......................... 105

    Dangers on the Frontier: "In the Name of the Lord of Hosts" 1754-1755 .......................................................... 108

    Edwards's Visit to Hadley—October 1756 .............................. 110

    Hadley: "The Light of God's Countenance"—October 1756 ...... 111

Edwards's Re-Preaching of Earlier Sermons ............................ 114

Jonah 3:10: Re-Preached 1756 ............................................... 115

Farewell Sermons to Stockbridge—January 15, 1758 ............. 119

Princeton: The Keys to Transitioning to a New Audience ...... 136

**CONCLUSION** ................................................................. 141

**BIBLIOGRAPHY** ............................................................. 147

New England Photos............................................................ 169

# PREFACE

Jonathan Edwards (1703-1758) is often known by many people from one sermon, "Sinners in the Hands of an Angry God." Additionally, he is stereotyped by many as a "monotone" and "manuscript preacher" who stared at the pages of his sermons and rarely looked at his audiences. What is not often understood is his life story and its connection with his preaching career.

Edwards is also often referred to as "America's Greatest Theologian and Philosopher." Although this may be true, Edwards's theology was "connected at the hip" with his preaching throughout his life. Edwards viewed his theology as something he was challenged to communicate through the spoken word. He believed that a preacher's theological knowledge should not be sheltered within the mind. He ardently believed that spiritual seeds were to be sewn and watered, and if God was willing, he would give "the increase" (1 Cor. 3:5-7, KJV). I argue that Edwards developed five distinct stages of communication development, and they remain relevant and applicable for contemporary utility. Instead of stereotyping and isolating events, there is an effort to look at Edwards's literary development in light of his entire life, along with the ups-and-downs, and to reveal his innovative ability to adapt and transition through the unpredictable events that come along with a life in the ministry.

Our insights into Edwards's life and works will introduce us to the major developmental stages of his career. We will present the major influencers early in his life and how these individuals influenced his understanding of communicating the Word.

His earliest manuscripts will be examined in relation to his later manuscripts, and also his semi-manuscripts and skeletal outlines. Further, we will discuss what each stage says about his methods and how each stage may have communicated characteristics of his delivery. Consequently, in the middle of his career, one particular influence may have changed his communication approach and played a role in the Great Awakening.

In the later stages of his career, we will look at one of the most traumatic events of his ministry and how this move may have forced him to adapt and transition into a complete new type of ministry unfamiliar to him. At this stage, Edwards continued to write major works, and we will expose how his years of experience and preparation methods impacted his publications and his teaching ability finally at Princeton. This study demonstrates the style in the eighteenth century, but at the same time connects concepts with twenty-first-century relevance with one of America's most intriguing preachers and theologians.

Toby K. Easley
Fort Worth, Texas

## ACKNOWLEDGMENTS

This book grew out of an interest in the life and sermons of a key figure in the First Great Awakening, Jonathan Edwards. The seminal ideas for the book stemmed from my 2007 paper presentation at the Evangelical Theological Society Regional Meeting held at Southwestern Baptist Theological Seminary in Fort Worth, Texas. Initial editing of the entire text in dissertation form was completed by the excellent work of Cathy Drewry of Fort Worth, Texas. During the writing process, Calvin Pearson, Ph.D., gave valuable advice and Robert W. Caldwell III, Ph.D., offered key resource recommendations. The Beinecke Library staff at Yale University provided outstanding assistance during my research visit. Ken Minkema, Ph.D., took time out of his busy schedule to answer my inquiries via e-mail related to the distinctive edwards.yale.edu website. Roberts Library at Southwestern Baptist Theological Seminary provided needed research materials for extended periods, and Tiffany Norris, Public Services Librarian, assisted with access to online research materials. Gwyn Snider at gkscreative in Nashville, Tennessee, proficiently designed the book cover and produced exceptional finishing touches for the aesthetic formatting. Finally, I want to thank my loving wife Kimberly for her patience and consistent encouragement; to her I dedicate this book.

# INTRODUCTION[1]

## *Jonathan Edwards*

### BEYOND THE MANUSCRIPTS

Jonathan Edwards toiled during his life to develop his sermon preparation and delivery.[2] Five developmental stages can be observed, extending from his youth to his first pastorate in New York in the 1720s, and continuing until his death in 1758. This book will seek to identify his five stages in chronological order by defining his early influences and the structural manuscript changes throughout his life. From this information, brief application suggestions for the contemporary will be presented. Furthermore, after identifying his early mentors, his manuscript alterations, and structural transitions; his communication mastery beyond the manuscripts will be explored.

---

1. Writer's note: Due to the historical nature of this book, the period quotes often contain archaic English spellings, grammar, and punctuations, or omissions of the same. In light of the frequency of these usages that any contemporary reader would consider as errors, in order to facilitate ease of reading, *sic* will not be used to denote errors of these instances.

2. Wilson H. Kimnach, *Works of Jonathan Edwards: Sermons and Discourses, 1720–1723* (New Haven, CT: Jonathan Edwards Center at Yale University, 1992), 10:3.

## Importance of the Topic

When individuals attempt to understand Edwards and his preaching, one characteristic needs to be understood from the beginning. He viewed his calling as a sanctified calling, and he set out from this early commission to give his best effort in developing his sermonic skills. His passion for preaching is evident in many of the sermons delivered to his congregations and his colleagues in ministry.

> To the person that is to be set apart to the sacred work of the gospel ministry this day: sir, I would now humbly and earnestly recommend to you that Holy Book which God is about to commit into your hands, as containing that message which you are to deliver to this people in his name. God gives you this word—which is his word—to preach that, and not the dictates of your own reason. You are to preach the dictates of God's infinitely superior understanding, humbly submitting your reason as a learner and disciple to that, renouncing all confidence in your own wisdom and entirely relying on God's instructions.[3]

In the last century, many have come to call Jonathan Edwards (1703-1758), of New England, one of America's greatest theologians. His preaching has stirred some controversy, not only from the perspective of doctrine, but also surrounding his communication abilities. One of his most read—and most famous—sermons is "Sinners in the Hands

---

3. Jonathan Edwards, "Ministers to Preach Not Their Own Wisdom but the Word of God," Sermons, Series II, *WJE Online* 55 (January-June 1740), Jonathan Edwards Center at Yale University [online]; accessed 16 December 2009; available at http://edwards.yale.edu; Internet. This was the ordination sermon for Edward Billing at Cold Spring (later Belchertown), Massachusetts. This sermon is important, because it gives Edwards's perspective on Reason and Revelation, his high view of Scripture, and the minister's responsibility to develop his preaching around God's inspired Word.

of an Angry God."⁴ Historically, he is often associated with the first Great Awakening of the 1740s, his father Timothy Edwards, grandfather Solomon Stoddard, Son-In-Law Aaron Burr Sr., grandson Aaron Burr Jr., friends George Whitefield, Samuel Buell, Samuel Hopkins, Joseph Bellamy, and John Erskine of Scotland.

Although Edwards's views on philosophy and science are often a topic of discussion, the fact that over twelve hundred of his sermons exist today provides a voluminous archive for significant discovery. For the twenty-first-century investigator of his works, not only do these sermons provide a historical treasure, they provide a vast supply of his concepts and development. As he became a preacher at a young age, he began to draft his sermon manuscripts in an octavo size that eventually developed into a duodecimo size.⁵ Additionally, one can compare these sermons with those of his father Timothy, who drafted manuscripts that, in some ways, mirror the manuscripts of his young protégé son.⁶ Kimnach describes Timothy's sermons as

> having three basic divisions of Text, Doctrine, and Application, each developed through a succession of brief, numbered heads. In a sermon of moderate length on Isaiah 26:9, Timothy Edwards employs no fewer than twenty-three numbered heads

---

4. Jonathan Edwards, "Sinners in the Hands of an Angry God," in *Works of Jonathan Edwards: Sermons and Discourses, 1739-1742*, ed. Harry S. Stout and Nathan O. Hatch, with Kyle P. Farley (New Haven, CT: Yale University Press, 2003), 22:400-418.

5. Wilson H. Kimnach, Introduction to "Literary Milieu," in *Works of Jonathan Edwards: Sermons and Discourses, 1720-1723*, ed. Wilson H. Kimnach (New Haven, CT: Yale University Press, 1992), 10:94-95. Kimnach believes that, for Edwards, the "duodecimo leaves would be easier to 'palm' in the pulpit." "Whatever his reasons, Edwards began using duodecimo leaves in 1727, and after a brief period when there are a few booklets of mixed leaves—such as Ps. 102:25-26—and an apparent vacillation between octavo and duodecimo booklets, he finally settled upon the duodecimo booklet of four-leaf signatures, and averaging twelve leaves per preaching unit."

6. The writer made these observations at the Beinecke Library, Yale University, September of 2009.

in the Doctrine and forty-four in the Application; moreover, many of these heads (averaging less than one hundred words each) contain numbered subheads within them. One does not move far without a "2dly" or a "3dly." The argument is abstract and unencumbered by imagery or metaphor; it is heavily laden with Scripture citations; the language is so "plain" as to be almost unnoticeable; the tone is forthright and serious, and the most obvious source of vitality is the frequent explicit references to men and events in the town. On the whole, it is a Puritan's Puritan form, and what it lacks in imagination and beauty in the superstructure, it makes up in the solidity of its foundation. The young Edwards could have done worse than sit beneath his father's pulpit if he wanted to learn the fundamentals of the traditional sermon form, for the classic Perkinsean virtues are embodied in the sermons preached there, without adulteration through imaginative innovation.[7]

Excitement and disappointment, as well as trial and error, characterized Jonathan Edwards's interesting life. First, in order to explore the full implications of Edwards's life surrounded by family, church, and people, the need exists to explore the historical dimensions surrounding his life and ministry. Second, to discover adequately his development as a proficient preacher, his manuscripts and outlines naturally will serve as a guide to his development and maturity.

Because Edwards was familiar with, and influenced by other members of his family who were in the ministry, the historical dimensions will shed light on the early impressions of his life. Not only was his father Timothy a Congregational minister, his mother had grown up in Pastor Solomon

---

7. Wilson H. Kimnach, General Introduction to *The Works of Jonathan Edwards: Sermons and Discourses, 1720-1723*, ed. Wilson H. Kimnach (New Haven, CT: Yale University Press, 1992), 10:11-12.

Stoddard's house, and was also the granddaughter of Pastor John Warham, the "controversial first pastor in Windsor."[8]

Furthermore, Edwards's enormous supply of material in his manuscripts provides voluminous information. Fortunately, at Jonathan Edwards's death, he left his sermon corpus in the hands of a trustworthy source. Edwards chose Samuel Hopkins to ascertain that his sermons were preserved. Additionally, Hopkins made a great contribution by writing a memoir of Edwards's life.[9] However, historical events often have a perplexing turn and for almost two centuries, the works and name of Jonathan Edwards were hushed, and the confines of Yale University held his sermons. A type of twentieth-century Edwardsean renaissance refocused scholars on the eighteenth-century preacher.[10] As a result, additional manuscripts have been placed in print, and a vast amount of new knowledge exists regarding Edwards's sermon form and sermon style.

Throughout this book, Jonathan Edwards's preaching will be examined from various contemporary angles. Not only was Edwards an able expositor, he was gifted as a writer and preacher. His ability in these two areas is attributable to his aptitude for balance in each area of his sermon preparation and creative methods. When juxtaposed with concepts today, Edwards's sermons seem to share many similarities and contemporary application. Furthermore, his motive to touch individual lives with the

---

8. George M. Marsden, *Jonathan Edwards: A Life* (New Haven, CT: Yale University Press, 2003), 23-24.

9. Samuel Hopkins, *Memoirs of Jonathan Edwards (1815)*, ed. John Hawksley (Kila, MT: Kessinger Publishing, 2009), 185.

10. Douglas A. Sweeney, "An Essay in American Religion and the Evangelical Tradition: The Legacy of Jonathan Edwards," *Taylorites, Tylerites, and the Dissolution of the New England Theology*, ed. D. G. Hart, Sean Michael Lucas, and Stephen J. Nichols (Grand Rapids: Baker Academic, 2003), 183. According to Sweeney, "the American scholarly community has witnessed a minor renaissance of interest in 'Edwardsian culture' during the past two decades, a renaissance located primarily among social and cultural historians of religion."

Gospel is what Bailey calls "an effort to connect with both the heart and the intellect of his auditors."[11]

With continued efforts to connect with today's audience, the need for exemplary sermonic methods remains relevant for those communicating God's Word. Perhaps the reason Edwards's stages remain applicable today is because God's Word remains relevant to people in every generation. Peter Adam wrote,

> God's revelation is both historical and contemporary. Our preaching of the Bible should not be merely historical (without contemporary application) or merely contemporary (with no regard to its historical context and meaning). Rather, we should reflect the two audiences God had in mind: the original hearers of the words, and those for whom the words are preserved, including ourselves.[12]

The same stands true for the need of sound sermon concepts and their usefulness from one generation to another. Consequently, the importance of this relevant information assists in keeping twenty-first century communicators from forgetting important individuals in the past, and aids in linking future generations with important sermonic concepts that should not be forgotten.

## Focus of the Topic

A primary goal will be to identify the five stages of Edwards's preaching, communication transitions, and manuscript development, while providing

---

11. Richard A. Bailey, "Driven by Passion, Jonathan Edwards and the Art of Preaching," in *American Religion and the Evangelical Tradition, The Legacy of Jonathan Edwards*, ed. D. G. Hart, Sean Michael Lucas, and Stephen J. Nichols (Grand Rapids: Baker Book House, 2003), 70.

12. Peter Adam, *Speaking God's Words* (Vancouver, BC: Regent College Publishing, 1996), 56.

some brief contemporary methods in which to apply his principles. Edwards preached on various topics and used vivid illustrations, theological content, and evangelistic strategies aimed at the local church. However, by abbreviating and sometimes combining his sermon notes and becoming more extemporaneous, he was able to improve his overall communication ability with his congregations and students. Kimnach calls one of Edwards's methods "recast" or "heavily revised."[13] As Edwards learned to adapt messages to his audiences, he would take an application section from one sermon and integrate it into another. Kimnach believes "Edwards fits the sermon to the audience and the occasion with the greatest care"[14] using this method. Additionally, he suggests that, in 1740, when Edwards heard Whitefield preach with a "spontaneous delivery," this caused Edwards to emulate him as best he could."[15]

Furthermore, an awareness of Edwards's developmental stages can be recommended as a plan of action in the contemporary. The knowledge of this material has the potential to teach and aid many today and propel them on a proper path to mastering Edwards's stages. This could have the potential of advancing one to a level of maturity in an accelerated manner by following the course of one of America's greatest preachers and theologians.

Within these developmental stages, one will also discover subjects that are relevant for the twenty-first-century communicator. The Church today should be interested in the theological and practical perspectives of Christians from other centuries. Through the voluminous manuscripts that he wrote and preached, Jonathan Edwards left us a vast resource on eighteenth-century sermonic development and theology.

Many of his stages of development and biblical subjects continue surfacing in present academic societies and theological discussions.

---

13. Kimnach, "General Introduction," 10:153.
14. Ibid.
15. Ibid., 122.

Furthermore, many of his sermon illustrations, theological descriptions, and practical applications can be quoted verbatim with modern effectiveness. Although Edwards changed his manuscript structure and approach over his career, his foundational theological perspectives remained rather static. Consequently, these valuable theological and literary resources possess the potential to contribute to numerous fields, stimulate further discussions, encourage more interest in Edwards's sermons, and benefit contemporary preaching now and in perpetuity.

## Outline of the Chapters

The chapters will explain the subject matter in the following order. The introduction section, followed by chapters 1-5, will present Edwards's development in chronological order and will describe briefly the practical concepts of Edwards's development that have contemporary application. Following chapter 5, the conclusion section will complete a wrap-up of his *Five Stages of Development*.

Chapter 1 will reveal the first stage of Edwards's communication development and how this stage began with auditory learning. Historians simply do not know all of the impressionistic moments that influenced the young pastor's son. This chapter will explore that, at a young age, Edwards sat through many months and years of preaching with his weekends saturated in the Gospel. From these early experiences, a rhetorical connection with his father and grandfather will be suggested by the literary similarities in their sermon notes. Following this historical examination of Edwards's early development, the chapter will conclude by presenting several categories that continue to offer opportunities for auditory learning today. Two that were available during Edwards's lifetime will be explored, and three categories that were not available during the eighteenth century will be briefly mentioned, due to Edwards's interest in new means of communication and scientific discoveries that potentially advanced homiletics.

Chapter 2 will reveal evidence regarding the manuscript stage of Jonathan Edwards's sermonic development and how this stage was more than likely conceived in his mind during these early years, resulting in the writing of his first full manuscripts. Not only will several of his first sermons be discussed, the physical attributes of the 1720's original manuscripts will be compared with later sermons. Obvious handwriting differences in early sermons will be described, and quotes by expert analysts such as Minkema will be offered. Furthermore, facts regarding the connection to the manuscripts and Edwards's delivery will be discussed for this early time period, and whether these early manuscripts have caused some to stereotype Edwards for his entire career.

The second part of chapter 2 will include emphasis on the importance of being able to write a sermon manuscript early in one's career and will describe the contemporary importance of being able to develop and maintain a sermon manuscript when appropriate throughout one's life. This section will not only encourage mastering and writing a sermon manuscript today, but it will also give three reasons why Edwards's manuscript phase was important then and now.

Chapter 3 will continue Edwards's journey beyond his first pastorate, through other brief ministries and educational experiences, which were followed by his calling to serve under his grandfather, Solomon Stoddard. During this period and following the death of Stoddard, outline forms appear as early as 1729 in Edwards's doctrine, application, and conclusion sections.[16] Chapter 3 will examine these sermons all the way through the 1730s and document this stage of development.

Even though many have said that Edwards never achieved an extemporaneous delivery, the second part of chapter 3 will draw conclusions from Edwards's changing approach and will reveal what those in the twenty-first-century can learn from the changing characteristics within Edwards's notes. Extemporaneity is not natural for most novice

---

16. Kimnach, Introduction to "Literary Milieu," 102.

communicators in the area of homiletics. Nevertheless, this chapter will briefly present some contemporary strategies through a modern plan to offer an efficient path to move practically from relying on the manuscript to developing a sound and effective delivery that mirrors Edwards's model.

Chapter 4 will open with the importance of the date beginning October 17, 1740, when George Whitefield made his way through the forest horse trails and crossed the ferry to Northampton.[17] Was this a life-changing experience for Edwards communication approach? Was this enough to persuade Edwards to change his style? This chapter will explore these and additional issues surrounding other manuscript structural changes and even skeletal outlines through the end of his Northampton ministry in 1750.

The second part of chapter 4 will discuss the skeletal outlines of Edwards and how they reveal a new communication attempt, even perhaps without an outline. Skeletal outlines pose a challenge for many communicators because of the absence of written information. In order for the contemporary communicator to relate to the five stages of development, the need to continue to improve external delivery is crucial. Was Edwards eventually able to preach without a skeletal outline or even memoriter? The writer believes the contemporary communicator has to be familiar with at least four elements in order to accomplish this practice. These four elements will be explained in the conclusion of chapter 4.

Chapter 5 will begin by introducing the period of ministry following his long Northampton, Massachusetts ministry and begin by discussing Edwards's overall maturity level in the fifth and final stage. Chapter 5 will review his new assignment in Stockbridge that forced him to learn new ways of communicating the sermon forms with which he was so

---

17. Iain H. Murray, *Jonathan Edwards: A New Biography* (Carlisle, PA: Banner of Truth Trust, 1992), 159, 161.

familiar beginning in 1751. The writer will present three characteristics that stand out in the Stockbridge sermons and why Edwards was forced to make these adjustments.

Chapter 5 will continue and introduce the period that led Jonathan Edwards to Princeton, New Jersey. The circumstances involved another president at the college, his own son-in-law. Was Edwards developed into the status of a master-preacher and communicator by this time, mastery being defined as one who has the ability to study for a sermon or lecture, write down a skeletal outline, and preach from his intellectual overflow by either glancing at the outline or preaching memoriter? The writer will conclude Edwards's life by describing this fifth and final stage as one of adaptation in Stockbridge and mature transition at Princeton. Additionally, answers will be offered to this question. Was Jonathan Edwards able virtually to adapt to diverse communication settings through his erudition by the time he settled into the College of New Jersey?

Chapter 5 will conclude by presenting brief contemporary suggestions for improving and developing transitional abilities in diverse settings. The keyword for this section will be adaptability. Once Edwards's maturation process is understood and practiced, the goal for those following Edwards's lead today should be the ability to adapt to various communication settings, including an educational environment. This final stage will conclude by offering a key area that Edwards understood and practiced in order to achieve maturity and an ability to transition to various communication venues.

The conclusion section will describe briefly the need for applying these principles today and how applying these stages could advance individuals to a level of maturity at various time rates, depending on isolated circumstances by following the course of one of America's greatest preachers and theologians. Finally, the writer believes all of these concepts are important in the twenty-first century, and that individuals should be interested in the theological and practical perspectives of the past and an ongoing concern about applying relevant practices in the present. Since many of Edwards's stages of manuscript development, communication style, and biblical subjects continue surfacing in academia, ecclesiological circles, and theological societies, these valuable discussions and new research have the potential to benefit contemporary communicators and shed light beyond his manuscript stereotypes.

CHAPTER 1

*Jonathan Edwards's*

AUDITORY LEARNING
AND DEVELOPMENT

Early in Jonathan Edwards's life, his sermonic development conceivably began with auditory learning as a young pastor's son. As he grew up in a minister's home, the frequency of time spent in church, as well as the repetition of sermons absorbed, could have made an impression on his young heart and mind. From what is known historically about Edwards's environment while being reared, it is possible that before he realized that God was going to call him to preach, week-by-week as the young lad sat in church and soaked in the words of his father Timothy, he was perhaps learning some of his manuscript structure and communication approaches as a protégé.

Perhaps the two most important influences upon Edwards' preaching style were his father and his maternal grandfather, Timothy Edwards and Solomon Stoddard, the former as a living exemplar of the preacher during his son's formative years, the latter as a master preacher to the young journeyman who shared his Northampton pulpit from 1726 to 1729. Edwards doubtless received his fundamental conception of the sermon form from his father, though Stoddard, a published critic of preaching, would certainly have suggested some master strokes to the preacher who was still developing his distinctive voice in the mid-1720s.[1]

Additionally, ministers in the eighteenth century were expected to be "hospitable," and when traveling preachers stayed in town, the pastor and his family usually welcomed them with open arms. One such occasion was the visitation of Stephen Williams, who came to hear Jonathan's father Timothy, during the awakening of 1715-1716. Murray says that Williams "would have found in Jonathan a receptive listener."[2] During those moments around the table, or in front of a comforting fire, the young preacher's son may have absorbed a type of divinity school through in-house discussions.

Describing the household of Jonathan's upbringing, Philip Gura said:
> The House as the years passed, Timothy added vestibules and ells to provide more space. Here Timothy prepared his sermons and instructed the young men who came to him to prepare for the ministry. He was particularly well regarded as a scholar in the classical languages and in Hebrew and at an early age his only son joined this tutorial, as did some of his sisters. Jonathan's parents doted on him as the only male heir, and his five elder sisters (particularly Mary, with her penchant for theology) shared their own growing knowledge with him as he prepared for what everyone expected, a career in the ministry. In this house, too, Timothy might have met with neighboring clergy to discuss and debate the ecclesiastical

---

1. Kimnach, "General Introduction," 10:10-11.
2. Murray, *Jonathan Edwards*, 21.

issues that animated the region. Although not a major participant in the church controversies that rocked the valley in the 1690's, Timothy, like many other younger clergymen, supported the recommendations of the Synod of 1662. . . . He resisted Stoddard's drive to open Communion to all morally upright townspeople and continued to examine prospective candidates for membership.³

Through this entire process, the Holy Spirit may have begun to consecrate the heart of a lad who would become one of America's brightest preachers and theologians. After all, young Jonathan had seen and experienced firsthand awakening in his father's congregation at a young age.

Turnbull said,

> The flowering of this experience as a lad came out of a home environment and he testified: "I had a variety of concerns and exercises about my soul from my childhood; but had two more remarkable seasons of awakening before I met with that change by which I was brought to those new dispositions, and that new sense of things that I have since had. The first time was when I was a boy, some years before I went to college, at a time of remarkable awakening in my father's congregation. I was then very much affected for many months, and concerned about the things of religion, and my soul's salvation; and was abundant in duties."⁴

Nevertheless, even though Jonathan's heart was stirred in these moments of awakening, he knew that his true conversion had not occurred. In his "Personal Narrative," he admitted while growing up he had "objections against the doctrine of God's sovereignty, in choosing whom he would to eternal life."

---

3. Philip F. Gura, *Jonathan Edwards, America's Evangelical* (New York: Hill and Wang, A Division of Farrar, Starus, and Giroux, 2005), 17.

4. Ralph G. Turnbull, *Jonathan Edwards the Preacher* (Grand Rapids: Baker Book House, 1958), 15-16.

## From Auditory Learning to the Written Sermon—A Father's Influence

When Jonathan Edwards was born to Timothy and Esther Edwards on October 5, 1703, he was to be the only son of eleven children. Not only was he the son of a preacher, he was the grandson and great-grandson of two other preachers.[5] Out of these three, naturally his father, Timothy, would be his preaching example during his formative years. Nevertheless, his grandfather, Solomon Stoddard, would also become an important part of his ongoing homiletical development in his young adult years. Although Timothy yielded a great impact on his son, it is also important to note that Solomon Stoddard's influence was possibly channeled to Jonathan through his father. Kimnach points to the sermons of Stoddard, and says, "they are reminiscent of Thomas Hooker," and that "the form of his sermons is the same as that used by Timothy Edwards."[6] Although this is probable, Jonathan later reduced his sermons, using fewer subpoints than his father had used.

The extant sermons of Timothy Edwards at Yale University carry a striking resemblance to those of Jonathan's. One of Timothy's sermons from the 1740s, taken from John 15:6 (KJV), is similar in appearance to Jonathan's later sermons in size and structure.[7] The importance of these existing Timothy Edwards sermons should not be underestimated when analyzing the homiletical impact upon his son. The external resemblances of Timothy's written sermons and Jonathan's sermons are

---

5. Gura, *Jonathan Edwards*, 18.

6. Wilson H. Kimnach, "The Sermons: Concept and Execution," in *The Princeton Companion to Jonathan Edwards*, ed. Sang Hyun Lee (Princeton, NJ: Princeton University Press, 2005), 250-51.

7. Timothy Edwards, A 1740's Sermon on John 15:6 (New Haven, CT, Beinecke Library, Box 24, Folder 1365). The writer observed this sermon at the Beinecke Library, in September of 2009. The size of this particular sermon was 4.5' X 3.5', and it has clear Text, Doctrine, and Application sections.

evident but not identical. Certainly, Jonathan had the utmost respect for his father who was well-respected as a scholar and member of the 1691 class at Harvard College.[8] As a curious son, it is highly probable that young Jonathan did observe his father's manuscripts and took note of every word, line, passage, and notation.

### From Auditory Learning to the Written Sermon—A Grandfather's Influence

Twenty-first-century Northampton, Massachusetts. remains a rather small town, with a bustling population that mixes locals with the Smith College students. On a hill above the cluster of churches, still stands Solomon Stoddard's home, referred to as the "Manse." Not only did Stoddard leave his mark with his home, his grave stands out among many in the local cemetery.[9] Stoddard expressed his disdain for lifeless preaching and said, "It may be argued, that it is harder to remember Rhetorical Sermons, than mere Rational Discourse; but it may be Answered, that it is far more Profitable to Preach in the Demonstration of the Spirit, than with the enticing Words of man's wisdom."[10]

As a young lad and later as a young man serving under his grandfather, Edwards would have seen and heard the passion with which his grandfather preached. Kimnach goes on to address conversion and claims that Stoddard and Timothy Edwards gave attention to "homiletical strategies

---

8. Helen Pelton, *Timothy Edwards (1669-1758)* (South Windsor, CT Library Board, a booklet published by South Windsor Historical Society, information compiled by staff of Wood Memorial Library, Spring 1968), 1.

9. On a trip to New England, in September of 2009, the writer visited the Northampton Cemetery, the Manse, and Edwards's old home site.

10. Solomon Stoddard, *A Plea for Fervent Preaching: The Defects of Preachers Reproved* (Boston: n.p., 1724), quoted in Kimnach, "General Introduction," 10:14.

that would promote this experience in their congregations."[11] Although young Jonathan was influenced in his sermon preparation and delivery by his close family, to him, he believed each individual preacher was transformed by God to preach with a "distinct charisma."[12] From what he had seen and heard, these individual distinctions applied to his father and his grandfather. Throughout his ministry, he chose to adopt sermonic forms from both of these men, but he also was independent in other ways as he developed many other creative forms in both sermon preparation, and sermon delivery.

## Contemporary Application of Stage One: Applying Edwards's Auditory Learning Stages and Development Today

Beginning with Edwards's auditory learning stage, many of those who are called to study and practice in the field of homiletics lack the opportunity to grow up attending church multiple times a week under their father's preaching. Nevertheless, for the contemporary analyzing the life and preaching of Jonathan Edwards, although multifaceted, in some ways, transcends the barrier of time due to many of his sound disciplined practices and sermon structure. Edwards was fortunate to have mentors from a young age and learned from observing and listening. Kimnach described this early auditory stage as "first in the home at his mother's knee and, later, at his father's tutoring school. There his education was focused, directly and indirectly, by the curriculum of Harvard College in the late seventeenth century."[13] Although Edwards was fortunate to have the background of his upbringing, many new opportunities for auditory learning are available today.

---

11. Ibid., 15.
12. Ibid., 21.
13. Kimnach, "General Introduction," 10:4.

Since the seventeenth and eighteenth centuries, things have changed drastically because of today's technological environment. Now the opportunity for auditory learning exists abundantly through modern technology and has gone far beyond the traditional modes that Jonathan Edwards could have imagined. Numerous categories continue to offer opportunity for contemporary preachers to attain auditory growth. Two from Edwards's lifetime consisted of local church mentoring programs and preaching events such as revivals. Several contemporary categories were unavailable during his lifetime and continue to offer ubiquitous opportunities for insight into homiletics. These consist of phone apps and internet sites, satellite and cable television, and satellite and local radio broadcasts.

## Local Church Mentoring Programs

During the eighteenth century, it was common practice for the local minister to also serve as a primary teacher and pastor within the community. Additionally, the ministers served as mentors for young men entering the ministry. Jonathan Edwards's pastor and mentor through God's providence was also his earthly father. Regarding this relationship Turnbull said,

> God has His own ways of preparing a life for special service. The cultured home and the attention given to an only son were factors of incalculable value in training the impressionable mind with those ideals and thoughts necessary for character. Out of the education of the home the boy was fitted for the more serious discipline of college training. His early years were years of mental growth, balancing the spiritual struggle of his inward being.[14]

Local church mentoring programs are not confined to the eighteenth century. Mentoring programs for those entering the ministry and those

---

14. Turnbull, *Preacher*, 13.

already in the ministry are still in use. For instance, some colleges and seminaries continue to require their students to work with a senior pastor or minister within a local congregation for credit hours. Some local churches voluntarily offer summer internships for young ministers to gain experience between semesters. Additionally, older adults entering the ministry may enter into training relationships with their pastor or staff following their personal surrender to the ministry. Consequently, these preaching and ministry-mentoring programs offer a plethora of opportunities for auditory and hands-on learning through the local church today.

## REVIVALS AND PREACHING EVENTS

The Church meetings, tutoring, and mentoring surrounding Jonathan Edwards's home and church apparently did not fall upon deaf ears. After a time of awakening in his father's congregation Edwards himself wrote,

> I used to pray five times a day in secret, and to spend much time in religious talk with other boys; and used to meet with them to pray together. I experienced I know not what kind of delight in religion. My mind was much engaged in it, and has much self-righteous pleasure; and it was my delight to abound in religious duties. I with some of my schoolmates joined together, and built a booth in a swamp, in a very secret and retired place, for a place of prayer. And besides, I had particular secret places of my own in the woods, where I used to retire myself.[15]

---

15. Jonathan Edwards, "Diary." In *Jonathan Edwards, Works of Jonathan Edwards: Letters and Personal Writings, Personal Narrative*, vol. 16, ed. George S. Claghorn (New Haven, CT: Yale University Press, 1998), 790-91.

This personal testimony regarding Edwards's childhood offers brief evidence for times of revival in the East Windsor years before the Great Awakening in the 1740s. Goen wrote that "seasons of spiritual concern in individual parishes, often intense enough to produce several converts for church membership, were not unknown in New England before the 'great and general awakening' of the 1740s."[16] These revivals and preaching events had an auditory impact upon Edwards at a young age, and reveal how learning and emotion are impacted by the spoken word.

Those involved in Bible teaching today should take note of these historical events. For one reason, contemporary outreach and preaching events may continue to serve as opportunities for growth. Not only can others' sermons offer instruction and growth through auditory, they can stimulate ideas for contemporary communicators to plan preaching events to reach people for Christ. Edwards was moved by the passion in the preaching he heard as a child, and this passion was passed on to the next generation through his sermons. Contemporaries need to realize they have a responsibility to influence the next generation through auditory. To Edwards, Spirit filled preaching was clear, confident, and stirring. Stott claims this is exactly what is perhaps missing in today's preaching.

> Without a clear and confident message preaching is impossible. Yet it is precisely this that the Church seems nowadays to lack. Not that this phenomenon is altogether new. Throughout Church history the pendulum has swung between eras of faith and eras of doubt. In 1882, for example, Macmillan published an essay by Sir John Pentland Mahaffy entitled The Decay of Modern Preaching. And at the beginning of this Century Canon J. G. Simpson of Manchester

---

16. C. C. Goen, Editor's Introduction to "The Great Awakening: A Faithful Narrative, the Distinguishing Marks, Some Thoughts Concerning the Revival, Letters Relating to the Revival, Preface to True Religion by Joseph Bellamy," in *Works of Jonathan Edwards: The Great Awakening*, vol. 4, ed. John E. Smith (New Haven, CT: Yale University Press, 1972), 4.

bemoaned the absence of authoritative preaching in England: "Not only does the race of great preachers seem for the time to be extinct, but the power of the pulpit has declined…. The pulpit of the present day has no clear, ringing and definite message." Small wonder that a child, wearied by a preacher's boring utterance, appealed "Mother, pay the man, and let us go home."[17]

Contemporary proclaimers should ask themselves whether they are impressing upon the minds and hearts of the next generation a passion for revival preaching or this "boring utterance" as Stott has bemoaned. Today, ministers should not only listen and learn, but additionally, they should prepare messages and proclaim them with passion, because the next generation is listening.

### Technological Advances in Biblical Communication

Forty years ago the word "apple" conjured up one image in the minds of English-speaking people—a circular red piece of fruit sometimes referred to as "Red Delicious" apples. However, in America's Bicentennial year of 1976, three young men—Steve Jobs, Steve Wozniak, and Ronald Wayne—started a new company named "Apple." If he had been alive, Jonathan Edwards might have made an eschatological sermon from the first market price of the Apple I computer, $666.66.[18] However, as the computer company developed into what has today become a mobile opportunity for theological learning, Edwards would have been pleased. Peter Theusen said,

---

17. John R. W. Stott, *Between Two Worlds: The Art of Preaching in the Twentieth Century* (Grand Rapids: William B. Eerdmans Publishing Co., 1982), 83.

18. *Wikipedia Online*, s.v. "Steve Jobs and Apple Computer" [on-line]; accessed February 2, 2012; available at http://en.wikipedia.org/wiki/Steve_Jobs; Internet.

Jonathan Edwards, who regarded all scientific advances as providential blessings, would no doubt erupt in spontaneous doxologies if he could return today and see that many of the eighteenth-century books he dreamed of obtaining are now readily available (with the right password!) in digital facsimile.[19]

## AUDITORY LEARNING THROUGH PHONE APPS

In the early 1990s, when the internet began spreading like wildfire and e-mail was taking off, who would have imagined that what began with a bulky home computer accessed via a modem would, in the twenty-first century, be carried in one's own pocket for instant information? Today with the Apple iPhone, written sermons, audio sermons, and sermon videos can be accessed through websites and YouTube. The writer has apps from several ministries on the iPhone, and uses them frequently while driving and studying.[20] Additionally, video sermons can be accessed through websites and YouTube using the same mobile phone or other type devices. Edwards's own sermon archive can be accessed through the internet through the iPhone and books read or heard.

## AUDITORY LEARNING THROUGH CABLE AND SATELLITE TV

Through cable and satellite television, sound auditory learning is available. As with any learning tool, pros and cons exist regarding

---

19. Peter J. Thuesen, *Works of Jonathan Edwards, Catalogues of Books, Note to the Reader* (New Haven, CT: Yale University Press, 2008), ix.

20. John MacArthur's website, Grace to You (www.gty.org) is one the writer frequently uses. He has the app downloaded on his iPhone.

preaching and television. Through the last several decades, scandals and abuses by televangelists have occurred. However, a vast opportunity has existed for ministers to use this medium for information, education, and observation. For instance, notes can be taken while listening to sermons on television, the homiletical outline evaluated, and illustrations gleaned.

Long before the age of television, Edwards was using vivid imagery. Contemporaries may continue to learn how he used imagery to paint pictures for his audience to impress images upon the minds of his listeners even in the age of television. Additionally, he used images to reach the human senses, whether through a reminder of "rain in time of drought,"[21] or seeking Christ as one seeks "silver or hid treasures."[22] In the sermon "Seeking After Christ," Edwards said,

> If you would find Christ, seek him as silver and search for him as for hid treasure. So we are directed to seek wisdom, Prov. 2:1-5. What pains do men [take] for the treasures that are hid in the earth: how do they dig and search; what hard labor do they undergo in digging for silver and gold and after earthly jewels. And if any man has lost some precious thing, how diligently and narrowly will they search for it? So diligently and earnestly seek Jesus Christ.[23]

In these illustrative words, Edwards challenged his audience to value Christ and their relationship with Him. Furthermore, by using the example of precious metals, he effectively constructed a visual image in order to stress the wisdom of seeking Christ.

---

21. Jonathan Edwards, "Like Rain Upon Mown Grass," in *Works of Jonathan Edwards: Sermons and Discourses*, 1739-1742, ed. Harry S. Stout and Nathan O. Hatch, with Kyle P. Farley (New Haven, CT: Yale University Press, 2003), 22:304.

22. Jonathan Edwards, "Seeking After Christ," in Works of Jonathan Edwards: Sermons and Discourses, 1739-1742, ed, Harry S. Stout and Nathan O. Hatch, with Kyle P. Farley (New Haven, CT: Yale University Press, 2003), 22:296.

23. Ibid.

## AUDITORY LEARNING THROUGH LOCAL AND SATELLITE RADIO

The first radio broadcast in the world occurred early in the twentieth century, and S. Parkes Cadman is said to be the first preacher to take his message to the airwaves in 1923.[24] Since that time, many others have taken the Gospel message to the airwaves and have even purchased their own radio stations such as KCBI in Dallas, the call letters representing the Criswell Bible Institute.

Today, pastors are spending on-average twenty hours a week commuting to work and home, to hospitals, church visits, conferences, and church functions.[25] These hours during a week offer further opportunities for auditory learning. Numerous ministries broadcast sermons, family counseling, and other audio choices via satellite and local radio. Even though things have changed dramatically since the eighteenth century when Jonathan Edwards preached the Gospel, multiple ways exist for individuals today to take advantage of modern technology, "redeem the time" and learn through auditory (Eph 5:16, KJV).

When the contemporary communicator analyzes Edwards's auditory learning stage, obviously many of those who are called to study and practice in the field of homiletics do not have the opportunity to grow up attending church multiple times a week under their father's tutelage. Jonathan Edwards was fortunate to have his background and upbringing in order to listen and learn more about effective communication. However, those who articulate Biblical truths today are fortunate to have new technological advances and opportunities for auditory learning. The contemporary Christian community not only can learn

---

24. *Wikipedia Online*, s.v. "S. Parkes Cadman" [on-line]; accessed February 2, 2012; available at http://en.wikipedia.org/wiki/Televangelism; Internet.

25. Car Insurance Comparison, "Clergy/Pastor/Bishop/Priest Car Insurance Rates" [on-line]; accessed February 2, 2012; available at http://www.carinsurancecomparison.com/clergypastorbishoppriest-car-insurance-rates/; Internet.

through a voluminous list of communicators that Edwards never could have imagined, but also many more technological mediums are available for individuals on the run. Through this access to auditory learning, one has the opportunity to expand knowledge while "out-and-about" in order to prepare better and communicate the Gospel to others who are also listening. As for Jonathan Edwards at a young age, he was the captive audience during his father and grandfather's sermons and whether he realized it or not at the time, he was soaking it all in with his photogenic mind. Their sermons he had examined in writing and their auditory deliveries captured in his mind would impact the first sermons he would eventually write and deliver.

CHAPTER 2

# Jonathan Edwards's
## DEVELOPMENT USING A FULL MANUSCRIPT

Traveling down I-95 in the twenty-first century, from New Haven, Connecticut, to New York City is a rather short drive. In Edwards's day, the trip was not so short and easy. Many traveled by water, and this would be the young preacher's new voyage for his ministry. After completing his baccalaureate degree with honors in 1720, Edwards would later deliver the valedictory oration on October 3, 1720. When the summer of 1721 arrived, Edwards experienced conversion at home in East Windsor. His "Personal Narrative" gives a detailed account of what he experienced.

> I began to have a new kind of apprehensions and ideas of Christ, and the work of redemption, and the glorious way of salvation by him. An inward, sweet sense of these things, at times, came into my heart; and my soul was led away in pleasant views and contemplations of them. And my mind was greatly engaged to spend my time in reading and meditating

on Christ, on the beauty and excellency of his person, and the lovely way of salvation by free grace in him.[1]

Edwards's salvation experience would make an impact on his preaching for the remainder of his life, especially on his passion to see others experience the light of the Gospel in their heads and the warmth of the Holy Spirit in their hearts.

Having assurance of his conversion, in the following August of 1722, Edwards left East Windsor to travel to New York City to "begin preaching to the English Presbyterian Congregation" on Wall Street.[2] The congregation had split over differences in the ideas of the Scot-Irish and the New-Englanders' ideas of Presbyterianism. The Scottish model was very strict, and the New Englanders accused the pastor, Rev. James Anderson, of ecclesiastical domination. The group to whom Edwards ministered met in a more modest structure, with both groups having a low number of parishioners.[3]

During this brief eight-month ministry, Jonathan Edwards drafted some of his earliest sermons. This environment was different from any he had ever faced, and Edwards had to make adjustments through his acquired homiletical journey in order to feed this splintered congregation with the Word of God. Edwards's days as a protégé helped him see sermon methods in practice, but now he was the practitioner. At this early stage, Edwards implemented a sermon method with which he was familiar, and he believed would work for this church. During this time, his structure went through minor changes, but precision for each situation and moment was what he sought. For the first time ever, Edwards was removed from his geographical comfort zone with his family at a distance. However, as he proved over the course of his life, Edwards lived up to the challenge.

---

1. Murray, *Jonathan Edwards*, 35-36.
2. Kenneth P. Minkema, *A Chronology of Edwards' Life and Writings* (New Haven, CT: Jonathan Edwards Center at Yale University, 1 [on-line]; accessed 18 December 2009; available at http;// Edwards.yale.edu/research/chronology; Internet.
3. Murray, *Jonathan Edwards*, 52-53.

## Jonathan Edwards's First Sermon in New York City

One of the first attributes of the 1720's original manuscripts, which is noticeable to the reader's eye, is the larger size of 6.25' X 3.75'. These are much easier to read than Edwards's later duodecimo-sized sermons. The text of Edwards's first New York manuscript is, "Say to the righteous that it shall be well with them, For they shall eat the fruit of their doings" (Isa 3:10, KJV).[4] The title of the message is "A Good Man Is a Happy Man Whatever His Outward Condition Is." Furthermore, the writing depicts a younger minister concerned with accuracy and readability from the pulpit. Minkema makes an accurate assessment by claiming, "During the New York and Bolton periods, Edwards neatly copied his sermons from drafts into prepared booklets; his handwriting was round and easily legible. But sermons composed at Northampton are written in a hand that is more slanted and hurried-looking."[5]

Other visual characteristics of the original manuscripts include words which Edwards wrote above some of the sentences at a later date in a lighter color ink. Perhaps Edwards added these notes to strengthen the sermon in a re-preaching. Additionally, in the Isaiah 3:10 sermon, Edwards used Scripture references from Matthew 5 which appear to be original to the sermon. However, Matthew 14:25 and Philippians 4 appear to be later insertions, and another obvious editorial is Romans 8:18, initialed by Jonathan Edwards.

In the final pages of the original Isaiah 3:10 manuscript, seemingly later insertions of Job 28 appear at the top of page twelve, along with a smaller, different type of paper, measuring 3' X 4' that has the appearance of a later

---

4. The writer observed the original manuscript from the first New York sermon, at the Beinecke Library, Yale University, September of 2009.

5. Kenneth P. Minkema, Preface to "The Period, 1723-1729," in *Works of Jonathan Edwards: Sermons and Discourses, 1723-1729*, ed. Kenneth P. Minkema (New Haven, CT: Yale University Press, 1992), 14:12.

insertion. The handwriting on this piece of paper is small and similar to the handwriting and paper color in the "Sinners" skeletal outline.

On pages thirteen and fourteen, a vertical line is marked through several paragraphs, which seems to indicate a deletion at a later preaching date. Edwards apparently deleted these paragraphs and added others on another small piece of paper. On page sixteen, the final page, a reference to Ephesians 2 appears original to the manuscript, but Kimnach does not have this verse as an original in his edited version. However, Kimnach appears to concur with this writer's observations by saying, "JE added the verse citations later."[6] Apparently, the verse citations Kimnach is referring to in his footnote are the ones he does not list in his edited version.

Regarding Edwards and his use of Scripture references, Miller uses Edwards's analogy as "an artist working in a tradition, and for him the tradition was sufficient."[7] In other words, like an artist, Edwards used the verses as if he were painting a picture. Consequently, the verses serve as color and appeal to draw in his audience from their experience, which causes them to place themselves within the picture itself in order to bring the imagery into real life.

As Edwards mastered his craft, his application sections evolved into historical masterpieces in sermons such as "Sinners in the Hands of an Angry God." On the other hand, Minkema saw Edwards's use of Scripture references as connecting points for future sermons. He accurately points out that, in the summer of 1729, Edwards's sermon on Job 31:3 makes reference to the phrase, "With the froward thou wilt shew thyself froward." He then points out that "within two or three

---

6. Jonathan Edwards, "A Good Man Is a Happy Man, Whatever His Outward Condition Is," in *Works of Jonathan Edwards: Sermons and Discourses, 1720-1723*, ed. Wilson H. Kimnach (New Haven, CT: Jonathan Edwards Center at Yale University, 1992), fn #2, 10:299.

7. Perry Miller, *Jonathan Edwards* (Toronto: George J. McLeod & William Sloan Associates, 1949), 48.

weeks, this very phrase appeared as the text for his sermon on Psalm 18:26."[8]

One of the characteristics of Edwards's sermons, which he maintained over the course of his life, was the three-section divisions of Text, Doctrine, and Application. One of the ways to identify an early sermon is the word "Use," instead of the later word "Application." On page nine of the original manuscript sermon on Isaiah 3:10, Edwards inserts the heading "Use" in this 1720's sermon, thus following the form of his father and grandfather. One of Timothy's 1709 sermons reveals the following organizational structure, "text, doctrine, propositions, and Use."[9] Although Timothy possibly taught young Jonathan much of his sermon structure, his manuscripts oftentimes have line-upon-line of propositions and other subpoints. Jonathan later condensed his outlines to avoid the congested look, and opted for a simpler format with "Text, Doctrine, and Application."

Furthermore, a marking that Edwards never abandoned in his sermons is the curved horizontal division line. However, in his earlier sermons, such as Isaiah 3:10, on pages six and seven, the line appears lengthier than in his later sermons.[10] Having been preached for the first time in New York City, Kimnach estimates this Isaiah 3:10 sermon possibly to "be the one he prepared for his licensing as a preacher and may even be his first formal effort in the sermon genre."[11] When compared to later sermons, the sermon does reveal some immaturity in

---

8. Minkema, Preface to "The Period, 1723-1729," 14:15.
9. John A. Stoughton, *Windsor Farmes: A Glimpse of an Old Parish* (Hartford, CT: n.p., 1883), 132.
10. Jonathan Edwards, "A Good Man Is a Happy Man, Whatever His Outward Condition Is (Isaiah 3:10)," *Writings of Jonathan Edwards*, Gen MSS 151, Box 13, Folder 994 (New Haven, CT: Yale University, Beinecke Library Rare Books and Manuscripts, 1720's Sermons).
11. Wilson H. Kimnach, Preface to "New York Period," in *Works of Jonathan Edwards: Sermons and Discourses, 1720-1723*, ed. Wilson H. Kimnach (New Haven, CT: Yale University Press, 1992), 10:283.

development. Edwards's transitions are not as smooth and, at times, his content seems redundant. Nevertheless, Edwards could have been appealing to the difficult circumstances which the people had experienced through the church split. In the conclusion, he told them,

> Go on, therefore, and forgetting the things which are behind, be pressing forward towards those which are before, even towards the mark for the prize of the high calling of God; and those afflictions will seem less and less to you, and your path will shine brighter and brighter, even till at length the night of this life shall be turned into perfect day, when God shall wipe away all tears from your eyes and there shall be no more death; neither sorrow nor crying, neither shall there be any more pain, for the former things will then be passed away.[12]

The second manuscript observed from this era is "The Gospel Dispensation Is Finished Wholly and Entirely in Free and Glorious Grace" (Zech 4:7). Kimnach has the sermon titled simply as "Glorious Grace."[13] The sermon manuscript is 6' X 4' with larger writing than the later duodecimo sermons. The name of Zechariah is written very large, and the text numbers are very legible. A line on the first page is marked out, the phrase "and indeed of the whole prophecy of Zechariah."

Formerly the wording was,

> the hope and design of the chapter and indeed of the whole prophecy of Zechariah, is to (comfort…is inserted) encourage the children of Israel returned out of the Babylonish captivity. In the building of the city Jerusalem the temple, who it seems

---

12. Edwards, "A Good Man Is a Happy Man," 10:306-07.
13. Jonathan Edwards, "The Gospel Dispensation Is Finished Wholly and Entirely in Free and Glorious Grace," in *Works of Jonathan Edwards: Sermons and Discourses, 1720-1723*, ed. Wilson H. Kimnach (New Haven, CT: Jonathan Edwards Center at Yale University, 1992), 10:390-91.

were very much disheartened, by reason of the opposition they met with in the work and the loss.[14]

Loss is marked out, and loss previously had a period after it, but Edwards substituted a comma and continued, "opposition they met with in the work of the excellence and glory of the former temple before the captivity. So there the priests and the gvnt and the Chief of the fathers, wept aloud." Additionally, Edwards uses the three-line division following his text in this sermon. He did not mark the doctrine section as such, but used very large letters saying, "Soe The Gospel Dispensation . . . Is." The word "Application" is written in large letters at the top of page twelve, and the backside of page ten (which is page eleven), is left blank. The final words of the sermon, on page seventeen, say, "Think and live God's praises."[15]

Another interesting characteristic about these early larger sermons is the way they were bound with one thread. The thread was tied in a knot on the inside middle pages, then looped in two threaded segments, entering the page 1.5 inches from the top of the manuscript, and 1.25 inches from the bottom of the manuscript. Edwards also did not use vertical column lines in this particular manuscript and the color of the paper is obviously not as dark as the Isaiah 3:10 and James 1:10 sermons.[16]

The content of this particular sermon (Zech. 4:7), has a sense of a special occasion. However, Kimnach mentions that, with this sermon, "one is tempted to link the sermon with the Christmas season merely on the basis of two references to the angels' singing at the birth of Christ."[17] The difficulty with this point of view is that Edwards and New England

---

14. The writer observed the original manuscript from the first New York sermon at the Beinecke Library, Yale University, September of 2009.

15. Ibid.

16. Ibid.

17. Wilson H. Kimnach, editor's comments on "Glorious Grace," in *The Works of Jonathan Edwards: Sermons and Discourses, 1720-1723* (New Haven, CT: Yale University Press, 1992), 10:388.

Congregationalists did not celebrate Christmas in the early eighteenth century, primarily due to its Catholic traditions. However, in New York, some individuals may have acknowledged Christmas, and Edwards simply made biblical references in order to emphasize Christ and his birth.

Furthermore, the sermon is very positive in tone and addresses man's sin and Christ's substitutionary atonement. Edwards preached,

> The fall of man brought it to this; it must be determined one way or t'other, and it was determined, by the strangely free and boundless grace of God, that this his own Son, should die that the offending worms might be freed, and set at liberty from their punishment, and that justice might make them happy. Here is grace indeed; well may we shout, "Grace, grace!" at this.[18]

Additionally, if men try to depend on anything other than the Gospel and God's grace, according to Edwards, they "set up themselves as the objects of it, as if their salvation at least partly, was owing to what they have done."[19] Therefore, those guilty of taking away from the grace of God cannot truly praise this "Glorious Grace." Thus, in order to emphasize this point in his conclusion, Edwards's crescendos into an alliterated chant, "praise him in prayer,…praise him in your closet,…praise him in singing…Surely, you have reason to shout, cry, 'Grace, grace, be the topstone of the temple!'…Wherefore, do nothing while you are alive, but speak and think and live God's praises."[20] Even among those who try to depict Edwards's preaching methods as "dry and stoic," one can surely imagine him raising his volume and increasing his tempo as he reaches his climactic moment, just like his father and grandfather, reiterating the subject of Divinity very dear to his heart, God's "Glorious Grace."

Nevertheless, skeptics will always exist who believe these early manuscript sermons naturally leave one with the assumption that Edwards,

---

18. Ibid., 393.
19. Ibid., 396.
20. Ibid., 399.

at this point in his ministry, actually lectured or read his manuscript. However, alluding back to his upbringing, he possibly was well ahead of his colleagues in both preparation and presentation. Nevertheless, Edwards was already attempting to master his delivery as quickly as possible. As with any young preacher, only time and experience in the pulpit can fulfill this desire. With the absence of any recording of his actual delivery, it is impossible to know whether he deviated from his manuscript at certain points. With a small amount of experience in a new congregation, Edwards more than likely moved carefully and methodically through his manuscripts in New York.[21] Thus, if a phase existed in which one could say, in relation to his delivery, that Edwards was strictly a manuscript preacher, perhaps it is this era. However, due to the absence of any verbatim recordings or modern recording devices, labeling him as a "stoic" or "dry" preacher is presumptuous.

Whether consciously or subconsciously, the images and mannerisms of his father and grandfather were with him in New York. They were his mentors, and although Jonathan would become his own man, some footprints existed in which he would walk his entire life, while other footprints he would avoid. The footprints he would be instructed to avoid were those of a lifeless, uninspired preacher, despised by Stoddard and the elder Edwards. For the young protégé, the called preacher was always experimenting with the sermon as a work of art, which meant that—with age—the landscape of his written sermons and delivery would potentially develop and be changed.[22] Additionally, the events of the 1730s and 1740s would influence his life and ministry. Some of his developmental changes appear in portions of his sermons and the adaptations that he methodically made. As each preaching environment changed around him, Edwards endeavored to rise to the occasion, as his art of preaching matured.

---

21. Kimnach, "General Introduction," 10:91-96.
22. Ibid., 41.

New York was a training ground, and he set out to make the best of every preaching opportunity, because he possibly speculated that when he arrived back home, everyone would analyze his communication progress from an external standpoint. Young Jonathan was not going to disappoint anyone; he desired to make the best out of every opportunity. In his personal resolutions that he started during his New York pastorate, he wrote in Resolution No. 30, "Resolved, to strive to my utmost every week to be brought higher in religion, and to a higher exercise of grace, than I was the week before,"[23] and that he did over the course of his life, leaving future generations a treasure of voluminous sermons that speak of God's glorious Kingdom within believers and His Kingdom yet to come. He more than likely was not satisfied with simply reading his sermons in New York; rather, he knew he could improve, and his mentors back home in Connecticut and Massachusetts were counting on it.

## Transition from New York to More Sermon Manuscripts at Bolton

During Jonathan's New York ministry, the elder Edwards was searching for a place for his son to serve closer to home. Some historians believe Timothy was concerned about the direction his son would go if he remained in New York. Perhaps Timothy was concerned that Jonathan might seek to travel overseas to England, and Timothy wanted to keep him in check until a permanent long-term position could be acquired closer to home. One can only imagine the exchanges taking place at this time between the Edwards's household at East Windsor and the Stoddard residence in Northampton with regard to young Jonathan's future.

During this time, Solomon Stoddard was in command of the

---

23. Steven J. Lawson, *The Unwavering Resolve of Jonathan Edwards* (Orlando: Reformation Trust Publishing, 2008), 160.

Northampton Church and perhaps, in his mind, he already had chosen his successor. However, for the moment, the two families had to be patient to see in which direction God would lead the youthful Jonathan. His mother, Esther (Stoddard) Edwards, at East Windsor, and his grandmother, Esther Stoddard, in Northampton, were keeping up with the protégé's future. The family had long since discovered the intellectual and spiritual potential of their young preacher.

By the first week in May, of 1723, Jonathan had returned from New York to East Windsor. From May until November, he was busy with two trips to Boston during June. During this period of July and August, of 1723, Jonathan Edwards worked toward completing his "Quaestio": "A Sinner Is Not Justified in the Sight of God Except Through the Righteousness of Christ Obtained by Faith." At New Haven, he delivered his "Quaestio," and received his Masters Degree.[24] Edwards laid out his "Quaestio" by declaring the importance of the doctrine, and then by defining what true justification is and its effects upon the individual. Just one year earlier, Edwards had been working on mastering his sermons in New York, but now he was sharpening his academic apologetics, while adapting to a new situation.[25] However, in just a short time, he would be working on his sermon skills again and preaching his manuscripts.

## JONATHAN EDWARDS AND THE BOLTON MINISTRY FROM 1723 TO 1724

By November 11, 1723, Jonathan Edwards had accepted his new position as pastor in Bolton, Connecticut, much to his father's pleasure. Timothy Edwards had written letters to Nathaniel Loomis, in Bolton,

---

24. Jonathan Edwards, "Quaestio," in *Works of Jonathan Edwards: Sermons and Discourses: 1723-1729*, ed. Kenneth P. Minkema (New Haven, CT: Yale University Press, 1992), 14:60.
25. Minkema, *Chronology*, 3.

with encouraging words about his son's intentions. One letter to Loomis in January, of 1723, said,

> I expect (life permitted & health continued) to see him in the spring and I am apt to think he will be here either in March or sometime in April next at furthest....I very much expect that he will leave the people with whom he now is at his next journey home. I have perused my Sons Letter to yourselves and find nothing in it Discouraging as to the motion you have made to him.[26]

On December 10, 1722, Jonathan wrote a letter, and the information is quite consistent with Timothy's letter of January 1723. Timothy's influence in the decision is quite evident.

> Gentlemen, According to my promise I here send you the most plenary and satisfactory answer that I can from the best observation and most mature deliberation I have been able to make since my return to New York. I have not been able to come to a full determination whether to leave York in a short time or No but I think for the present considering the circumstances of the Society and my Fathers inclination to the contrary, it seems most probable I shall not settle here, but am ready to think I shall leave them in the spring. I believe I shall not return into New England till that time. Whither you will wait with expectation of me so long is entirely with you and as you think fit. I think it would be unreasonable of me to desire or expect it of you, especially considering that it is not absolutely certain that I shall leave York then. This is all the Resolution Gentlemen that I can possibly give you at this time. I assure you I have a great esteem of and affection to the people of your Town so far as I am acquainted with them, and should count it a Smile of Providence upon me if ever I should be settled amongst such a

---

26. Stoughton, *Windsor Farmes*, 84.

People as your Society seems at present to me to be. I heartily wish for your Prosperity in all things especially upon spiritual accounts, that God would give you an able, faithfull, Pious, and succesfull Pastor, that may be a Great Instrument of the advancement of Gods Glory & the Eternal interests of Souls among you. I am your hearty friend & humble Servt, Jonathan Edwards.[27]

The church was considering two candidates for the position. The favorite candidate was Edwards, and if he declined, the intentions were to call Isaac Stiles of Westfield. The town records from October 10, 1723, give the following information:

At a town meeting in Bolton legally warned Oct 10, 1723 voted at said meeting to give the Rev. Mr. Edwards in case he should settle in the work of the ministry in This Towne the allotment in Bolton assyned by the comtt for the Ministry with all the rights appertaining thereto. Voted also to give him the sum of 220 pounds for his settlement, and salary for the space of two years, commencing from his first coming among us and settling in said town.[28]

Later in the month, on October 28, some other details were given about the ministry in Bolton:

Voted that the town shall take the whole care of gathering the Rate and that the minister shall have nothing to do but to receive it, and if the minister shall agree with any person to do any work, or pay his Rate in provision he shall give a note. Voted also that the Rate the three years shall be 60L the next year 65 L the next 70L, the next 75 the next 80L. Voted also that all the male inhabitants of Bolton from 16 years old and upwards work two days in each year for the three years in fencing and clearing

---

27. Ibid.
28. Ibid., 81.

for the minister. Voted that the ministers Rate of salary shall be paid annually one half in money, and the other half in Indian corn & wheat at current money price. Voted also that the people shall cut and cart the minister's wood. Nov. 9, 1723, Voted to add to the said salary of 80L per annum when there shall be occasion, and as shall be just and reasonable.[29]

Edwards's brief ministry in Bolton is not filled with vast amounts of information. Some have speculated that the community had a divisive spirit. Others have said his passion for a "lovely girl, the daughter of an eminent New Haven clergyman, threw her weight in the scale that preponderated in favor of Yale, thus turning from the comparatively obscure country town into the congenial ways of thought and culture the studious man whose companionship she afterward shared."[30]

Edwards recorded some thoughts about this young lady by writing:

They say there is a young lady in _____ who is beloved by that Great being who made and rules the world, and that there are certain seasons in which this Great Being in some way or other invisibly comes to her and fills her mind with exceeding sweet delights, and that she hardly cares for anything except to meditate on him. That she expects after a while to be where he is, to be raised up out of the world and caught up into heaven, being assured that he loves her too well to let her remain at a distance from him always. There she is to dwell with him. Therefore if you present all the world before her with the richest of its treasures she disregards it and cares nothing for it and is unmindful of any pain or affliction. She has a strange sweetness in her mind and singular purity in her affections, is most just and conscientious in her conduct, and you could not persuade her to do anything wrong or sinful if you would give her all the world, lest she

---

29. Ibid., 82.
30. Ibid.

should offend the Great Being. She is for wonderful sweetness calmness and universal Benevolence of mind Especially after this Great being has manifested himself to her mind. She will sometimes go about from place to place singing sweetly and seems to be always full of Joy and pleasure, and no one knows for what. She loves to be alone walking in the fields and groves and seems to have someone invisible always conversing with her.[31]

This certainly sounds like a passionate young man who is having difficulty focusing on his ministry. Nevertheless, the thinking is that Edwards re-preached many of his New York sermons during this time at Bolton. "Of the twenty extant sermons from the New York period, nine have an asterisk, the Bolton repreaching symbol, on them. However, several others that are not marked with an asterisk contain revisions that may date from the Bolton period."[32] Even so, these months were not in vain, for they certainly offered Jonathan the opportunity to refine his delivery, work on ministerial skills, and to live close enough geographically to spend quality time with one of his mentors.

One of the interesting dynamics of Timothy desiring his son to serve at Bolton is regarding the people. The Bolton area had been recently settled, and many of its inhabitants were from East Windsor and Windsor. At East Windsor, Timothy had struggled at times because of the lack of financial support from his own congregation, and he must have known that many of these folks would treat his son no differently. Although Timothy's salary was supposed to be paid in money, due to the poverty of some of the parishioners, he often had to settle to be paid through different means, such as food and clothing.[33]

When going to Bolton, the twenty-year-old son may have had reservations, due to knowing the way some of these same people had treated his father. Nevertheless, he felt duty-bound to listen to the counsel of his

---

31. Ibid., 82-83.
32. Minkema, Preface to "The Period, 1723-1729," 14:5-6.
33. Stoughton, *Windsor Farmes*, 54-55.

father, and to grit his teeth and bear all for God's glory. Marsden is probably accurate when he says, "taking this modest position near to home seems to have been mainly his father's idea."[34] Seemingly, young Jonathan would find a way to get out of the situation and find his way back to New Haven. On May 21, 1724, he was elected as Tutor at Yale. By the end of May, he had left Bolton. By the first week in June, he was ready to start his tutorship.[35]

Between May, of 1724, and August, of 1726, when he was asked to assist Solomon Stoddard at Northampton, Edwards's preaching duties appear sparse, although evidence exists that he preached some former sermons in Glastonbury, Connecticut, from April to July of 1726. Other opportunities probably presented themselves; however, history is sometimes silent on various details that historians wish they could acquire. Nevertheless, several items of interest are known for certain. By October of 1726, Edwards would begin to serve in Northampton alongside his Grandfather Stoddard, and by July 28, 1727, he and the love of his life, Sarah Pierpont, would be joined in marriage. He more than likely was not satisfied with simply reading his manuscripts that he had already preached, and he knew his grandfather, Solomon Stoddard, would hold him to a higher standard.

## Contemporary Application of Stage Two: How to Develop a Manuscript Using Edwards's Model

Although a full manuscript is often one of the first written forms some inexperienced communicators use in preparation, the importance and relevance of maintaining an ability to write and utilize a manuscript over time remains a contemporary point of discussion. Although Edwards developed and used the full manuscript early in his career, he continued to make changes and reductions. However, for very important speaking

---

34. Marsden, *Jonathan Edwards*, 95.
35. Minkema, *Chronology*, 3.

events, Edwards continued to produce a full manuscript perhaps for several reasons. First, Edwards enjoyed writing and being involved in apologetics. Second, perhaps he desired his messages for important events, funerals, ordinations, and so forth, to be passed on to the next generation, and so he intended to pass his written sermons to the care of Samuel Hopkins in the case that Edwards preceded him in death.

Ilian Jones described this type of future intention as, "some ministers... compose their sermons for a future reading public rather than the present listening public."[36] However, Edwards seemed concerned and interested in communicating to both the present and future. Third, although Edwards worked throughout his ministry to become a more extemporaneous communicator, perhaps due to his detail-oriented personality, he wanted to make sure not one word was left unspoken or forgotten for these momentous occasions. Fourth, Edwards may have believed that occasionally going back to writing an occasional full manuscript kept his preaching sharp. Finally, evidence is certain regarding one static aspect of his sermon forms throughout his entire career, and that was his emphasis upon the Text, Doctrine, and Application (Use) structure.

## The Contemporary Relevance of the Manuscript

Therefore, not only will individuals today be encouraged in the following pages to master writing a manuscript, but three reasons will be given why the manuscript needs to be mastered early in one's communication journey. First, the manuscript encourages one to think through the material and to write out the thought process clearly. Second, the written material enhances the memorization process by writing out the full text in its entirety. Third, writing a proficient manuscript lays the foundation for the future in becoming a better extemporaneous speaker. In other words,

---

36. Ilion T. Jones, *Principles and Practice of Preaching* (Nashville: Abingdon, 1956), 170.

repetition and experience in writing and delivering manuscripts usually increases confidence in being able to glance at the main ideas in the overall outline and eventually achieve more extemporaneity.

## Manuscript Philosophies

How Jonathan Edwards actually wrote—and then preached his manuscripts early in his ministry, is the model that will be referred to for this subject. However, a brief acknowledgement regarding other philosophies and how manuscripts should be written in relation to the homily needs to be recognized. Some individuals stress writing the manuscript following the delivery. They claim this will cause the speaker to be more conversational over time with this exercise. In other words, the first presentation of the oral delivery is, therefore, not bound by a verbatim written copy. Consequently, the written manuscript's utility would be for the benefit of those who would read their own content following the delivery and develop a conversational tone. This process is perhaps made simpler in the twenty-first century than it was in the eighteenth century because of modern technological recording. Chappell suggests this model for the written sermon: "A sermon, being a spoken address, ought to sound spoken. The minister who first prepares and preaches his sermon, then writes it, is more likely to attain this end. Such a minister writes as he speaks instead of speaking as he writes. Thus his sermon seems spoken even when read."[37]

Chappell has a valid point, but many who write oral presentations on a regular basis realize that his suggestion is much easier said than done, especially for inexperienced presenters. However, the exercise could prove effective by analyzing the differences in the written manuscript and the spoken words, and his ultimate goal seems to be the development of a consistent homily—both in the written and spoken form through analysis

---

37. Clovis G. Chappell, *Anointed to Preach* (Nashville: Abingdon Press, 1951), 85-86.

and use. Although Chapell is advocating a written manuscript sequence with a variance from Edwards's approach, contemporary communicators may wish to consider both of these approaches and discover which one has the best utility for them.

## OTHER IMPORTANT DYNAMICS TO CONSIDER IN RELATION TO THE MANUSCRIPT

Particularly for an experienced communicator, the delivered message often has interjected phrases and words the speaker did not premeditate before the actual delivery. A sermon recorded from the speaking event does give future generations a more accurate and realistic idea of what the audience heard and sensed in that day and time. For instance, Charles Spurgeon's secretary hand-recorded his spoken sermons. A valid historical and homiletical question is, if only Spurgeon's written outlines were available, or even the manuscripts he wrote at a young age, how would this change the perception of his communication style to those who never witnessed his preaching?

Chappell's point is valid, but also brings to light the fact that Edwards wrote his sermons before speaking them, and he did not have a secretary recording his actual delivery word-for-word. Contemporary historians and communicators may wish to ask the question then, would Jonathan Edwards's sermons be perceived differently today if a handwritten form of his actual delivery was available? Perhaps the answer to this question will never be known. However, this information should encourage individuals to have an open mind when considering the suggestion of this book, that Jonathan Edwards's preaching was not static over the course of his life, and to follow his example of preparing a sermon manuscript before initial delivery has contemporary utility, especially early in one's ministry. However, other manuscript approaches such as Chappell's are worthy of consideration, because research and experimentation in sermon development does bring healthy results over the course of time.

## WRITING A SERMON MANUSCRIPT PROVIDES CLARITY

One of the benefits of disciplining oneself to write out sermon manuscripts early in ministry is that the process usually produces a clearer thought process for the sermon delivery. Vines and Shaddix suggest, "the young preacher would do well to discipline himself to write out at least one full sermon manuscript per week during the early years of his ministry. Such was the practice of the great expositor Lloyd-Jones."[38] If Jonathan Edwards and Lloyd Jones both believed early in one's ministry the manuscript was vital and important, perhaps contemporary preachers should take note.

As time constraints increase and schedules become packed with events and meetings, writing one manuscript out of three sermons a week is a worthy goal. The repetition of the exercise will make a difference over time as experience is gained in the life of the herald. Kroll gives some other "advantages" and "disadvantages" to the sermon manuscript,

> The manuscript method has several advantages. The speaker can deliberate over the exact words he wants to use. He can provide more accurate facts to support his case. He can predetermine the length of his sermon. The speaker can have greater excellence of style, being more precise, concise, and concrete. The sermon is in written form so it can be retained for delivery on another occasion or even published. The speaker has a greater freedom from speech fright for the words he is to say are written before him . . . disadvantages to this method for a busy pastor, writing out several sermons in full each week saps time from

---

38. Jerry Vines and Jim Shaddix, *Power in the Pulpit How to Prepare and Deliver Expository Sermons* (Chicago: Moody Press, 1999), 202.

other pastoral duties. The speaker also tends to become dependent on a written manuscript every time he is asked to speak. It is an effort simply to write out each sermon which adds to the difficulty. The speaker is compelled to follow the plan of the speech and can only with great difficulty stray from it. As to delivery, this method is probably the least effective. Eye contact is almost obliterated. Again, reading a manuscript tends to lessen the amount of gesturing and emphasis that a speaker can use.[39]

## How Memorization Is Enhanced by the Manuscript

Memorization is enhanced by writing a manuscript in two ways. First, the writing process aids in memorization as the sermon is crafted. However, those who memorize verbatim do increase the time of preparation involved for one sermon. One alternative to this laborious option is what Vines and Shaddix call "free delivery."[40]

One of the biggest complaints people make about their pastor is that he uses a manuscript or notes. Constantly looking down at his paper hinders the effectiveness of his delivery. Certainly, some men can use a manuscript or sermon notes quite well. They have developed techniques that enable them to rely upon some form of written sermon help without making it noticeable. Most preachers, however, never develop such an ability. Consequently, the best way to deliver expository sermons is to use no notes at all. This approach is called free delivery. Many of the great preachers in the Christian faith have used the free delivery method. Alexander Maclaren prepared for each sermon very

---

39. Woodrow Michael Kroll, *Prescription for Preaching* (Grand Rapids: Baker Publishing Group, 1980), 116.
40. Vines and Shaddix, *Power in the Pulpit*, 340.

carefully. Actually, he prepared more carefully than if he were planning to read the message or speak it from memory. Then he allowed the words to well up from his heart at the moment of delivery. G. Campbell Morgan, that "Prince of Expositors," also used this method. . . . Free delivery is characterized by the preparation of a full or partial manuscript, complete familiarity with the written material by identity instead of memory, and delivery of the sermon without the use of the notes.[41]

Writing the manuscript is a way of aiding in the memorization process, but as this "Prince of Expositors" exemplified, the existence of the manuscript does not necessarily mean one must read it in the pulpit. Writing the manuscript serves a purpose, but one main purpose is to etch the content upon the heart and the mind for a memorized, smoother delivery.

Second, once the sermon is written in full, a repetitious reading of the manuscript enhances the memorization process. The outline of the major divisions will become clearer, along with the explanation of the text, the doctrine and illustrations, and practical application. In other words, the overall thought process and flow of the sermon will be imprinted visually upon the messengers mind and heart. This repetitious process will seem arduous to an inexperienced individual; however, the process itself over time may prove to be a worthy exercise. Eventually, the repetition of this overall method may naturally produce a reduction in the amount of time that needs to be spent as memorization strategies will be mastered, and preparation time substantially reduced. Furthermore, improvements in moving from dependence on the manuscript to a "free" or "extemporaneous" approach may be reached. Jonathan Edwards began as a "manuscript" preacher, but suggestions will be presented that he improved over time as he moved through his five stages of development, working toward the ability to speak more extemporaneously beyond the manuscripts.

---

41. Ibid., 340-41.

CHAPTER 3

## *Jonathan Edwards's*
## PROGRESSION FROM THE MANUSCRIPTS TO OUTLINE FORMS

The three years following Edwards's Bolton ministry were spent as a tutor at Yale, along with other writing activities such as his "Notes on Scripture," in 1724, and additions to the Miscellanies. Additionally, from April to July, in 1726, he preached periodically in Glastonbury, Connecticut.[1] One of his "heavily travelled" sermons, preached in Glastonbury, was titled "The Pleasantness of Religion," a sermon Edwards preached in Bolton and Northampton as well.[2] In August, of 1726, a request was made for Edwards to assist his grandfather, Solomon Stoddard, at the Northampton, Massachusetts church. Thus, he resigned his tutorship

---

1. Minkema, *Chronology*, 3-4.
2. Jonathan Edwards, Introduction to "The Pleasantness of Religion," in *Works of Jonathan Edwards: Sermons and Discourses: 1723-1729*, ed. Kenneth P. Minkema (New Haven, CT: Yale University Press, 1992), 14:98.

in September. On October 26, of the same year, he started preaching as probationer and was ordained as the Northampton assistant pastor on February 15, 1727.[3]

Almost two years later to the day, Edwards became the senior pastor when Stoddard passed away, leaving the leadership with his young protégé. Jonathan Edwards now had the responsibility of filling some large shoes. This awesome responsibility, and his strenuous work ethic, possibly led to Edwards's illness. He was out of the pulpit for two months before finally returning to his flock, where he received a warm welcome upon his return.[4]

Now, Edwards was ready to settle in and place into practice all of the preparations that had been made in the past. Northampton was his pulpit for the next twenty-one years, but the road ahead was not without tribulation. From 1749-1750, one of his New York sermons on Isaiah 3:10 would be put to the test in his own life to see whether he could practice what he preached.[5] He had followed what he believed to be God's will, to be a pastor rather than a formal educator at Yale. He followed the paths of his father, Timothy Edwards, and his Grandfather Stoddard in pursuing the kingdom of God as a passionate practitioner of preaching but with his own creativity.

The idea of a plurality of "homiletical strategies" regarding Edwards is not intended as a hyperbolic statement. Edwards became a visionary, anticipating God to stir the hearts of people. He was not afraid to use versatility in his delivery to expand God's kingdom. Regarding preaching and revival, he believed,

> Our people don't so much need to have their heads stored as to have their hearts touched and they stand in the greatest need of

---

3. Minkema, *Chronology*, 4.
4. Murray, *Jonathan Edwards*, 94.
5. Jonathan Edwards, "Christian Happiness," in *Works of Jonathan Edwards: Sermons and Discourses, 1720-1723*, ed. Wilson H. Kimnach (New Haven, CT: Yale University Press, 1992), 10:296-307.

that sort of preaching that has the greatest tendency to do this. Those texts, Isa. 58:1, "Cry aloud, spare not, lift up thy voice like a trumpet, and shew my people their transgression, and the house of Jacob their sins"; and Ezek. 6:11, "Thus saith the Lord God, smite with thine hand, and stamp with thy foot, and say, alas, for all the evil abomination of the house of Israel!"—I say, these texts (however the use that some have made of them has been laughed at) will fully justify a great degree of pathos, and manifestation of zeal and fervency in preaching the Word of God. They may indeed be abused, to justify that which would be odd and unnatural amongst us, not making due allowance for difference of manners and custom, in different ages and nations; but let us interpret them how we will, they at least imply that a most affectionate and earnest manner of delivery, in many cases, becomes a preacher of God's Word.[6]

Additionally, in over two decades in Northampton, Edwards was unique in his ability to ingest information from multiple sources and consistently filter that information through his biblical worldview. After reading *Freedom of the Will*, Mark Twain called him "a drunken lunatic" and a "resplendent intellect gone mad."[7] Conversely, McClymond claimed, "Edwards, in short, was God intoxicated."[8] Therefore, one observes these vast differences of opinions among writers in relation to his intellect, as well as his preaching methods. Nevertheless, Edwards desired discernment in his preaching that was balanced objectively and subjectively. He continuously analyzed his content, structure, and delivery—not only to

---

6. Jonathan Edwards, "Some Thoughts Concerning the Revival," in *Works of Jonathan Edwards: The Great Awakening*, ed. John E. Smith (New Haven, CT: Yale University Press, 1972), 4:388.

7. Mark Twain, "Letter to Rev. Joseph H. Twitchell" (February 1902), in *Mark Twain's Letters*, ed. Albert Bigelow Paine (New York: Harper, 1917), 2:719-21.

8. Michael J. McClymond, *Encounters with God: An Approach to the Theology of Jonathan Edwards* (New York: Oxford University Press, 1998), 29.

please his fathers in the ministry, but primarily to please his heavenly Father.

Eleven years into his Northampton ministry brought an overpowering voice from England that would captivate his mind and bring him to tears. The late 1720s and the entire decade of the 1730s brought change, variation, and maturity into the preaching of Jonathan Edwards. He had grown up under Timothy Edwards's ministry, even though eventually as a young man he learned directly under Stoddard. However now, he was at a distance from East Windsor, and Solomon Stoddard was gone on to his heavenly reward.

## THE DEVELOPMENT OF EDWARDS'S EARLY PREACHING

Pastors, like Edwards, who consistently preach on a long-term basis, understand that a journey exists in one's own sermon preparation and preaching style. In Northampton, Edwards's sermon preparation and presentation was not totally static. His Text, Doctrine, and Application approach remained in place, but the ebb-and-flow of his preaching and life story was anything but static. Events and people, and God's surprising movement among the churches, convinced Edwards to remain steadfast in principle, but to utilize flexibility in practice. Edwards desired to be the best in every circumstance, and he sought ways to improve his content and delivery.[9] Consequently, his sermon notes reveal changes over time while he was in Northampton. One of his weekly passions was his ambition to fulfill the charges of his father and grandfather before his ascent into the pulpit, which was to impress the sermon into the hearers' hearts.

Hosts of preachers like Edwards have prepared sermon manuscripts. However, the manuscript itself does not reveal the rhetorical pathos of the delivery, but rather the spirit-filled man of God reveals it. Edwards

---

9. Murray, *Jonathan Edwards*, 189.

understood that the only way one can accomplish this dynamic is by the supernatural ability that comes from God. During his Northampton pastorate, Edwards was striving to maintain precision, while becoming more extemporaneous, and his manuscripts do not prove that he was a monotone, stoic, lifeless preacher, as some have laid claim. Rather, his manuscripts reveal a young preacher who desired to address circumstances with God's Word, in order to maximize his ability to communicate the Gospel with detail and biblical reason. Regarding Edwards's principles, Bailey said:

> Even though he both knew the work of the great philosophers of his day and affirmed their concept of the important role of human reason, he did not share their conviction of the primacy of human reason. Most advocates of the Enlightenment championed reason over divine revelation. Edwards, however, defended the traditional protestant notion of revelation both in theory and practice.[10]

## Northampton Preaching from 1729 Through the 1730s

Following the death of his Grandfather Stoddard, Edwards set out, in 1729, to prepare his sermons with efficiency and precision. Additionally, outline forms appear in the Doctrine, Conclusion, and Application sections.[11] This marks a new beginning in his preaching, and perhaps contradicts the image of the Northampton preacher that Peter Marshall depicts:

> In 1734, the lightning began to strike America. As the place for the first bolt to fall, God chose Northampton, Massachusetts,

---

10. Bailey, "Driven by Passion," 65.
11. Kimnach, "General Introduction," 10:102.

the little town of the most learned and respected theologian which America had yet produced. Jonathan Edwards was a brilliant, but reserved, dry Puritan preacher, who delivered his sermons in a monotone, with his eyes never straying from the back wall of the church.[12]

However, Marshall's statement ignores three important factors.

First, by 1729, Edwards had completed two years of working under Stoddard. He disapproved of preachers who read their sermons in a dull way. Second, by 1729, Edwards was already beginning to use more outline forms. Third, Edwards's friend, Samuel Hopkins, did not deny that Edwards sometimes read from his notes, but he made a point to say that "he was not confined" to his notes, and that "he would deliver them with as great propriety and fluency, and often with greater pathos," so as to have the maximum effect upon those who were present.[13] Further, Hopkins's account of Edwards's passion is consistent with his actions during the 1730s. As God began to move upon his congregation, Edwards made every effort to kindle, rather than stifle, the fire. During this first awakening time in 1734-1735, his sermons reflect a preacher who desired people to recognize their sinful conditions, repent, and turn to God.

When Edwards took over the Northampton pulpit, one of the issues pressing on his mind was the European controversy stemming from the end of the seventeenth century regarding the Trinity.[14] More than likely, he started preaching "The Threefold Work of the Holy Ghost," in April

---

12. Peter Marshall and David Manuel, *The Light and the Glory* (Old Tappan, NJ: Fleming H. Revell Co., 1977), 241.

13. Samuel Hopkins, *The Life and Character of the Late Reverend, Learned and Pious Mr. Jonathan Edwards, President of the College of New Jersey, Together with Extracts from His Private Writings and Diary*, 1st ed. (Northampton, MA; reprinted Puritan Reprints, 2007), 52.

14. Jonathan Edwards, Introduction to "The Threefold Work of the Holy Ghost," in *Works of Jonathan Edwards: Sermons and Discourses, 1723-1729*, ed. Kenneth P. Minkema (New Haven, CT: Yale University Press, 1997), 14:371.

1729.[15] This would have been two months following Stoddard's death, and Edwards was most certainly feeling the pressure of being thrown abruptly into the role of sermonic soloist. He was in the process of establishing himself as the minister of the Northampton congregation. By June, of 1729, these pressures most likely played a large role in his poor health. Minkema's claims are evidence to the fact that, by this time, he was trying to utilize his time and become more precise and efficient in his sermon preparation:

> The style of the sermon marks a transition for Edwards. Perhaps due to the demanding and lengthy nature of the discourse, he used abbreviations more than ever before. While parts of the discourse are fully written out, others are written in a sometimes terse, sometimes fragmentary manner. Scattered sections amount to nothing more than lists of points contained in mere words or phrases meant to be expounded extemporaneously. The uneven nature of the sermon's composition may reflect Edwards' increasingly poor health, which resulted in a debilitation in June. Taken as a whole, however, this composition suggests that Edwards was also experimenting, not so much with changing the formal structure of the sermon itself, but with his own powers of memory and association, as well as with how to produce sermons more efficiently.[16]

Further, as previously cited, this evaluation is consistent with Kimnach, and the evidence from the original manuscripts is consistent with the above description. Static characteristics to Edwards's sermons are present, but time and paper were scarce commodities, and efficiency and increasing brevity within his notes remained important to him as well as continuing to improve his sermon delivery. Time and experience were naturally making a change in Jonathan Edwards's note structure and delivery, because maturity

---

15. Ibid.
16. Ibid., 374.

is a natural process for those who prepare and preach homilies every week. This structural and rhetorical process he worked through continues to simulate the sermon maturity of those in the twenty-first century as well.

## Contemporary Application of Stage Three: Drawing a Contemporary Model for Outline Forms

Even though Jonathan Edwards continued to move toward more outline forms, it is important to emphasize that he did not completely abandon writing manuscript sermons. His sermons do reveal that he began to experiment and then implement condensed versions of his full manuscripts in the late 1720s and early 1730s. This continues to offer a contemporary model for developing outline forms.

Three contemporary strategies will be suggested through a modern plan, to offer an efficient path practically to move from relying on the manuscript to developing a sound extemporaneous delivery. First, every effective communicator should be able to develop a semi-manuscript that leads to a skeletal outline. Second, after mastering the manuscript and semi-manuscript, as recommended in the previous and present chapter, one may strive to ingest and digest information and then be able to speak from the heart by glancing at the skeletal outline. Third, as confidence and ability are attained with the extemporaneous delivery, the individual should strive for discipline to remain focused on the topic at hand. Edwards was very good at staying on the substance of his content, and the contemporary plan should follow the same course.

## Developing the Semi-Manuscript into a Skeletal Outline

Having discussed the importance of the full manuscript in the previous chapter, following Edwards's model, the semi-manuscript takes the sermon to a more abbreviated form. When an individual has reached a certain comfort level with the full manuscript, the semi-manuscript offers less clutter and more abbreviated thoughts. Depending on the section of the sermon, some sections may offer more opportunity for brevity than others. For instance, for the explanation of the text sections, more complete thoughts may be necessary. However, the illustration sections may be a section where a single word or short sentence is used to trigger the memory. Additionally, the application section may offer abbreviated thoughts and ideas depending on the extent of the application.

Over time, moving from full manuscript to the semi-manuscript, to a skeletal outline takes time, but often is a natural product of experience and hard work. Typically, adept communicators will know the time is right to move from one phase to another. To move straight from a full manuscript use to a skeletal outline could cause stress and ineffectiveness during delivery of the content. A semi-manuscript offers an intermediate phase where the "meat of the matter" is present but does not contain the subject matter word-for-word. Edwards's sermons during the 1730s contain these types of brief explanations, along with periodic notations as reminders to him during the preaching event.

## Delivering the Message from a Skeletal Outline

Once the semi-manuscript is mastered, some individuals like to move to a skeletal outline. A skeletal outline usually states the title, text, and main points of a sermon, and may also give some brief words for the introduction and conclusion. Moving into a skeletal outline phase of one's approach may take fifteen to twenty year's time depending upon the comfort level. A copy of Edwards's "Sinners in the Hands of an Angry God" sermon exists in manuscript and skeletal outline form at the Beinecke Library.[17] If the date of the outline was close to the date of the 1741 manuscript, Edwards would have been close to a twenty-year veteran by that date. Additionally, he would have preached hundreds of sermons throughout that span of years, and possibly felt quite comfortable using the skeletal form with certain sermons.

In contemporary terms, Vines and Shaddix also include the skeletal form within the scope of their "free delivery."

> While preaching, the preacher uses no written notes other than maybe brief notations in his Bible or a skeletal outline on a small sheet of paper. The logical flow of ideas clearly is established. The sequence of ideas is the same as the prepared written material, but the choice of the particular words may vary at the time of delivery.[18]

An excellent benefit exists with this maturity level. Kroll gives an excellent description of the benefits of the skeletal outline and the ability to communicate well.

> This method of delivery requires the preparation of a thorough but flexible outline, without writing out the contents verbatim.... There are definite and obvious advantages to this method. The extemporaneous method requires far less preparation than the memorization or manuscript methods. Less time is needed because of the quality of preparation, not because of the amount of preparation. One spends as much time in gathering and correlating material in this method as he does in the others. Time is saved, however, in that the material does not have to be written out in full. Further time is saved in that the speaker does not have to

---

17. The writer observed the "Sinners" outline and manuscript on a visit to the Beinecke Library, Yale University, September of 2009.

18. Vines and Shaddix, *Power in the Pulpit*, 343.

memorize verbatim this material. This allows the busy pastor to deliver a sermon with good content on Sunday and still have time to do his calling throughout the week.[19]

Delivery from a skeletal outline is a noble desire for any messenger; however, knowing when you are ready to use this method is also very important. It is vitally important because of the eternal significance of the Gospel message. Every time a preacher stands to preach, he does not know who in his audience might be listening to his or her last sermon.[20] Steven Smith describes the importance of preaching in his book:

> Make no mistake about it—preaching is a powerful medium. Think about it. Here you are with a congregation of people in front of you—some are facing God's judgment for their sin and don't even know it, while still others have at best a warped sense of Christianity. All that stands between you and this gathered crowd is a book. And you stand, like it or not, as an authority on that Book, telling them what God says about ultimate questions.[21]

Consequently, moving from one stage type to another during one's career needs to be considered with much prayer and consideration. When the transition does occur from one stage to another as Edwards did, the main focus should be awareness of the readiness to move to a more advanced mode of communication regarding the greatest Gospel message entrusted to men.

---

19. Kroll, *Prescription for Preaching*, 118-19.
20. Through years of ministry, the writer has had experiences where people in his congregation have been in church on Sunday and due to illness or other events passed away within several weeks. This is not only a reminder of the brevity of life, but also of the importance of the message one preaches.
21. Steven W. Smith, *Dying To Preach: Embracing the CROSS in the PULPIT* (Grand Rapids: Kregel Academic and Professional, 2009), 47.

## Skeletal Outlines and a Focused Approach

One of the qualities of Edwards's manuscripts is the way he remained focused throughout the course of the message. There is no way of knowing for certain if Edwards always maintained this intense focus, or if he occasionally strayed from the topic— especially when observing his skeletal outlines. Nevertheless, for the contemporary spokesman, this is a worthy goal to maintain focus upon the sermon topic as extemporaneous ability is attained.

One of the potential weaknesses of using the skeletal outline is the "disadvantage of straying. The extemporaneous speaker sometimes has a tendency to follow a red herring."[22] All who communicate through speaking have at one time or another fallen victim to their own "straying."[23] One way to monitor focus upon one's topic is to evaluate the presentation through recording. Listening to one's own sermon or speech can be humbling. However, an ongoing critique of content, presentation, and focus should exist. Haddon Robinson said,

> Students of public speaking and preaching have argued for centuries that effective communication demands a single theme. Rhetoricians hold to this so strongly that virtually every textbook devotes some space to a treatment of the principle. Terminology may vary—central idea, proposition, theme, thesis statement, main thought—but the concept is the same: an effective speech "centers on one specific thing, a central idea.". . Homileticians join their voices to insist that a sermon, like any good speech, embodies a single, all-encompassing concept.[24]

Additionally, staying focused on the topic will make the sermon more interesting. The thoughts will remain tied together, and people are also

---

22. Kroll, *Prescription for Preaching*, 119.
23. Ibid.
24. Haddon W. Robinson, *Biblical Preaching: The Development and Delivery of Expository Messages* (Grand Rapids: Baker Book House, 1980), 33-34.

less likely to complain about the length of the sermon. H. W. Beecher once said, "The true way to shorten a sermon is to make it more interesting."[25] For those in the past such as Edwards, and those who present sermons in the future, focus and continual improvement in delivery are important. Throughout the 1730s, Jonathan Edwards progressed in his developmental stages, and several events beginning in the 1740s influenced his perception of an "Awakening" sermon. He may have experimented with skeletal outlines and extemporaneous preaching in the 1730s, but his virtual concept of the term "extempore" was soon ready to be expanded as he observed a great communicator who had already moved beyond the manuscripts in his early twenties.[26]

---

25. Henry Ward Beecher, *Lectures on Preaching: Personal Elements in Preaching, the 1872 Yale Lectures* (London: Nelson, 1872), 257.

26. Kimnach, "General Introduction," 10:124.

CHAPTER 4

# *Jonathan Edwards's*
## TRANSITIONS FROM THE GREAT AWAKENING UNTIL 1750

On October 17, 1740, George Whitefield made his way through the forest horse trails and crossed the ferry to Northampton.[1] When Whitefield stepped to the pulpit, one of the most impressive orators of Colonial history stood to speak, and one of the greatest minds sat in the audience and "wept during the whole time of exercise."[2] The power in the preaching of Whitefield must have been overwhelming for Edwards. Ben Franklin once calculated that Whitefield "could be heard by as many as thirty thousand in an outdoor setting."[3]

Was this a life-changing experience for Edwards homiletically? The emotional response of Edwards during the sermon reveals how his

---

1. Murray, *Jonathan Edwards*, 159, 161.
2. Ibid., 162.
3. Marion Aldridge, "George Whitefield: The Necessary Interdependence of Preaching Style and Sermon Content to Effect Revival," *Journal of the Evangelical Theological Society* 23, no. 1 (March 1980): 59.

heart was stirred. The interior walls of the modest-sized meeting house in Northampton must have trembled with a preacher who could be heard by a multitude outdoors. Was this enough to persuade Edwards to change his preaching style? Ralph Turnbull said, "he had the homiletical gift of structure,"[4] which was certainly true, but even Turnbull leaves questions about the certainty of Edwards's dullness of preaching by saying, "if there was little of the surprise element in Edwards's way of preaching and little variation in the form of the sermon, it was because he was steeped in the Puritan Tradition."[5] Once again, the "Puritan" stereotype is applied to Edwards, albeit in an uncertain mode. Analyzing the hermeneutics of Edwards, Samuel T. Logan Jr. wrote, "Edwards was one of the leading preachers and theologians of the Great Awakening. As such, he participated and even led the homiletical revolution."[6]

If a "little of the surprise element" was present in his preaching, this meeting with Whitefield might have begun to change his perspective. The Great Awakening did begin to bring about a new homiletical approach to preaching, and little doubt exists that George Whitefield played a role.

Throughout his journeys, Whitefield urged ministers and aspiring ministers to "preach without notes," and criticized recorded written sermons as a deficiency in faith: "I think the ministers preaching almost universally by note, is a mark that they have, in great measure, lost the old spirit of preaching. Though they are not condemned who use notes, yet it is a symptom of the decay of religion, when reading sermons becomes fashionable where extempore preaching did once almost universally prevail."[7]

---

4. Turnbull, *Preacher*, 107.
5. Ibid.
6. Samuel T. Logan, "The Hermeneutics of Jonathan Edwards," *Westminster Theological Journal* 43 (1980): 87.
7. Harry S. Stout, *The New England Soul: Preaching and Religious Culture in*

This was not a new concept for Edwards, because his grandfather had said similar things in his *Defects of Preachers Reproved*. Stoddard had given him the model, and Whitefield exemplified the model. Perhaps this is why Kimnach said, "the thought arises that Jonathan Edwards, under the influence of Whitefield, might have made an outline of his Northampton sermon for the Enfield performance."[8] He does point out that the ink in the extant outline does not match that particular timeframe.[9]

Nevertheless, this fact does not negate the mere possibility of Edwards using an outline for the sermon of July 8, 1741. After all, just nine months earlier, Whitefield had held the Northampton congregation spellbound during his sermons. Sarah Edwards, in a letter to her brother, the Rev. James Pierpont, said, "It is wonderful to see what a spell he casts over an audience by proclaiming the simplest truths of the Bible. I have seen upwards of a thousand people hang on his words, with breathless silence."[10] From 1740 until his death in 1758, the development of Edwards in improving the utility of the sermon not only reveals that he did not need to lean wholly upon the manuscript, but it may confirm the impact of Whitefield and his desire for spontaneity. Kimnach has some compelling observations:

> The outline sermon of the forties is often much less of a sermon than an earlier sermon would be if it were reduced to an outline. It just does not have as many essential parts. The shift to outline sermons has been explained in the past in several ways, but the most frequent explanation is that

---

*Colonial New England* (New York: Oxford University Press, 1986), 357-58, quoted in Jim Ehrhard, "A Critical Analysis of the Tradition of Jonathan Edwards as a Manuscript Preacher," *Westminster Journal of Theology* 60 (1998): 73-74.

8. Kimnach, "General Introduction," 10:145.

9. Additionally, the writer noticed the ink variation when observing the "Sinners" outline on a visit to the Beinecke Library, Yale University, September of 2009.

10. Murray, *Jonathan Edwards*, 162.

Edwards "had mastered the pulpit." This is an improbable analysis. Edwards had surely mastered the pulpit by 1735 when he led the first widely publicized awakening among his own people and preached some of his finest sermons, and he had gained all the mastery he was ever to have over the sermon form by 1727. More plausible is the notion that Whitefield, whom Edwards met and heard preach in October 1740, impressed Edwards with his "spontaneous" delivery and caused Edwards to emulate him as best he could.[11]

Granted is the fact that, by 1735, Edwards had mastered much regarding the "sermon form." However, in 1735, he still had miles to go before reaching his communication pinnacle.

## Northampton and the "Sinners" Sermon

To those who have read one of Edwards's most famous sermons, "Sinners in the Hands of an Angry God," the story behind the sermon may go unnoticed. Edwards first preached the sermon with little effect at Northampton in June, of 1741, but the great response to the sermon came when Edwards preached the sermon again at Enfield, on July 8, 1741. This sermon not only has a surviving manuscript, but also a complete outline of the sermon written by Edwards. The previously mentioned date, of 1729, found Edwards using minor internal outlines in his sermons. As Edwards grew older, this practice became more prevalent. Kimnach says the "Sinners" sermon was not only preached numerous times, the sermon went through various revisions. After being revised for print, the sermon was approximately the same as the original manuscript except for the "last three-sevenths of the sermon."[12]

---

11. Kimnach, "General Introduction," 10:121-22.
12. Ibid., 113.

The printed version was a compilation of all of the previous drafts, and the application section ended up with new content and was very different.[13] All of these multidimensional aspects to Edwards's preaching, writing, and publishing of sermons reveal his desire to develop every dynamic of communication. If this same creativity carried over into his preaching pathos, boxing him in as a stoic manuscript preacher is to limit the man who sometimes pressed the limits.

The allegations of extremes in Edwards's life go in opposite directions from his delivery to accusations of manipulation. First, is the claim of Clark's comment regarding Edwards staring while preaching, "he looked on the bell rope until he looked it off."[14] Second, as a revivalist, did Edwards manufacture a setting that he knew would produce an emotional outburst? In his article on "Radical Revivalism," Doug Winiarski, goes to another extreme, suggesting that Edwards took advantage of what he calls "mystics" across the river in Suffield. These young people, who he says had "experienced raptures in the form of dreams, trances, and visions," were a part of the audience for the Enfield sermon. Edwards wanted it that way to "engineer the dramatic response."[15]

Certainly, the possibility for some of the more radical "New Lights" to have intervened is not beyond possibility. However, for Edwards to seek out and manipulate a group of charismatic "mystics" is, in this writer's opinion, a major miscalculation,[16] especially in light of

---

13. Ibid.
14. Miller, *Jonathan Edwards*, 51.
15. Douglas L. Winiarski, "Jonathan Edwards, Enthusiast?: Radical Revivalism and the Great Awakening in the Connecticut Valley," *Church History* 74, no. 4 (December 2005): 709, 729.
16. Gura, *Jonathan Edwards*, 106-07. Gura says, "After Buell's visit Edwards was troubled by his increasing inability to control such behavior." One incident involved Edwards's wife Sarah, who wrote, "My soul remained in a kind of heavenly elysium." Jonathan would later say, "When people were raised to this height, Satan took the advantage." Further, Gura goes on to say that, in order "to capitalize on the ongoing revival," Edwards "sought to control its excesses."

Edwards's later responses in rebuking those who took the awakening to excesses.[17] In reality, who was this preacher from Northampton, in 1741, and did George Whitefield and the events of 1740 change his preaching forever?

## EDWARDS'S DEVELOPMENT OF SERMON NOTES

The changes during the late 1720s reveal that Jonathan Edwards had experimented with his preaching preparation and delivery in his past. However, his tenacious attitude of perfecting both for the future is obvious. In his earlier days, he used an octavo sermon booklet that measures approximately 6.25' X 3.75', with other similar ones from the 1720s measuring 6' X 4'. Additionally, he later changed to the duodecimo booklet that measured approximately 4' X 3.75' in the 1730s, with variations in the 1740s at 4.5' X 3.5'.[18] The pages were normally stitched together with a small thread,[19] and the earlier

---

17. Jonathan Edwards, Personal letter to Deacon Moses Lyman, May 10, 1742, in Jonathan Edwards, *Letters and Personal Writings, Personal Narrative*, ed. George S. Claghorn (New Haven, CT: Yale University Press, 1998), 16:101-02. In this letter, Edwards addresses one of the problems that had arisen regarding "Lay exhortation," and the problems associated with this new practice. "My Dear Friend, I am fully satisfied by the account your father has given me, that you have lately gone out of the way of your duty, and done that which did not belong to you, in exhorting a public congregation. . . . If God had not seen it necessary that such things should have certain limits and bounds, he never would have appointed a certain particular order of men to that work and office, to be set apart to it, in so solemn a manner, in the name of God. The head of the church is wiser than we, and knew how to regulate things in his church."

18. The writer made these observations of Edwards's sermon dimensions at the Beinecke Library, Yale University, September of 2009. The measurements were carefully made with a ruler, and further discussion on this can be found in chapter 2 of the book, on the New York ministry of Jonathan Edwards. Additionally, Kimnach, "General Introduction," 10:95, gives a picture of the different sizes.

19. The thread is visible in Kimnach's picture in "General Introduction," 10:95.

sermons had used a horizontal line going across the page, but now the vertical line would separate the page.[20]

The duodecimo was divided into either four, six, or even eight small squares resembling the size of a postage stamp. Additionally, they are referred to as his "thumb notes" or his "palm notes."[21] Thus, they were able to be held in the "palm" and read without being aesthetically distracting. Kimnach gives a picturesque idea of these notes:

> By adding the vertical line in the center of the page, he divided the roughly four-inch-square duodecimo page into four, or more often six and sometimes eight, little squares—each square presenting a writing area the size of a postage stamp. And, as one might expect, as the years pass the writing tends to recede from all four margins of the box, until, in many sermons of the late forties there are only a few words huddled at the center of each box. Moreover, these alterations signal still further alterations, for during this period the sermon itself becomes less and less of a literary structure.[22]

## NORTHAMPTON 1742 SERMON ON HEBREWS 12:29

This is a sermon that was observed in its original written form and is entitled "God Is Himself the Fire that Shall Destroy and Consume Wicked Men," from the text, "For our God is a consuming fire" (Heb 12:29, KJV).[23] The sermon is a duodecimo size, and the paper is similar in

---

20. Ibid., 121.
21. Ibid.
22. Ibid.
23. Jonathan Edwards, "God Is Himself the Fire that Shall Destroy and Consume Wicked Men (Heb. 12:29)," Jonathan Edwards Collection, MSS 151, Box 14, Folder 1128 (New Haven, CT: Yale University, Beinecke Library, May 1742). The writer examined this sermon at the Beinecke Library, Yale University, September of 2009.

color with the "Sinners" skeletal outline sermon. This sermon is a visual example of Kimnach's description, with a vertical line spanning the entire page and the horizontal lines dividing the segments of the sermon. The handwriting is typical of Edwards's skeletals from this period, and the handwriting is much more difficult to read than the 1720s manuscripts.

One legible reference of 2 Thessalonians 1:8-9 exists on page nine, and the sermon consists of eleven total pages. The marking of Text, Doctrine, and Application sections are visible, and the date is clear. Two threads hold the pages together in the middle of the left margin, and they run through the holes twice, with a knot that is apparent on the front page. He used the symbol with a circle and a dot in the middle once. This is the symbol Jonathan and Timothy Edwards both used as an abbreviation for the word "world."[24]

This sermon certainly exemplifies the diminished "literary structure" Kimnach cites. However, the more important sermons of the 1740s are an example of Edwards returning to his former ways of preparing a detailed manuscript. Important events, such as his ordination sermons, guest lectures, and difficult situations at Northampton, exhibit this tendency, along with his "Farewell Sermon"[25] in July 1750. Naturally, these tendencies do seem to reflect a man who is diverted with a multifaceted life and ministry. However, by the mid-1740s, Edwards had over twenty years of preaching experience. The possibility exists that he had the confidence, even with the momentous manuscript sermons, to "preach extempore."[26] In essence, by the mid-1740s, Jonathan Edwards was on a quest for preaching proficiency.

At this point in Edwards's life, his erudition was a blessing, but the time to accomplish all that he desired was pressing him. He was gifted in multitasking, but as he became more confident in the pulpit, he also

---

24. For the abbreviations and the translations used by Timothy Edwards, see Stoughton, *Windsor Farmes*.
25. Kimnach, "General Introduction," 10:124.
26. Ibid.

knew that he could prepare his sermons and still find time to publish other works. Additionally, he had to maintain his pastoral duties and his role as a husband and father. After the first Great Awakening, his popularity had spread, and Edwards now tried to fit every aspect of his life into his already overburdened schedule. He was not immune to the difficulties and criticisms of being a pastor, and Ola Winslow's critical remarks mirror some of the weaknesses of Edwards's personal life. She wrote that "twenty years in the pulpit had taught him nothing about the delicacy of human relations."[27]

However, what Winslow perhaps overlooks is the fact that Jonathan Edwards was always more concerned about proclaiming the truth and his potential to offend God by not being a faithful herald. Edwards was actually sensitive to the "delicacy of human relations," and voiced his concerns in a 1744 ordination sermon:

> Avoid contention among yourselves about your own temporal affairs. This will exceedingly tend to render a minister's labors ineffectual; and it is what greatly damps the spirit and discourages the heart of a minister, to see his people divided into parties, and envying one another, and entertaining mutual prejudices, jealousies and grudges, and so backbiting and reproaching one another, and carrying on secret plots and designs one against another.[28]

The delicate matter that would plague Edwards later in the 1740s would involve people, but the actual problem was moral and doctrinal in nature. Naturally, people would be involved, but a matter of church discipline regarding a midwives book, and changing a major doctrine

---

27. Ola Winslow, *Jonathan Edwards 1703-1758* (New York: Collier Books, 1961), 204.

28. Jonathan Edwards, "The Great Concern of a Watchman for Souls," in *Works of Jonathan Edwards: Sermons and Discourses, 1743-1758*, ed. Wilson H. Kimnach (New Haven, CT: Yale University Press, 2006), 25:80. This sermon was an ordination sermon for Mr. Robert Abercrombie, preached in Pelham, 30 August 1744.

that his Grandfather Stoddard propagated, would bring the death blows to Edwards's Northampton ministry and preaching. Furthermore, the death of his uncle, John Stoddard, in June of 1748, removed a figure of strength, which had supported Edwards's ministry.

Colonel Stoddard had headed the selection committee that sought Edwards as an associate of Solomon Stoddard. As divine providence would have it, Jonathan Edwards would end up later in Stockbridge, the township that Colonel Stoddard laid out, in 1736, on the Housatonnuck, where he had helped to establish an Indian mission. Although Stoddard did not know it at the time, he was indirectly involved in the last pastorate for his nephew, although he would never live to see it happen.[29]

In the future, Edwards would be faced with a homiletical challenge he had never faced before. He would be involved in two congregations, one an English-speaking, the other a Mohican-speaking Indian congregation. The former he preached to in their dialect; the latter he preached to through an interpreter. A future question for Edwards would be, could he overcome the homiletical obstacles? Second, is Kimnach correct in affirming that the period between "1727-42 is that in which Edwards achieved mastery of the sermon"?[30] Certainly many developmental and communication hurdles were lying in the future for the 1750s.

## Northampton Preaching: Edwards's Homiletical Development Continues

Although this period of the 1740s is not saturated with as many manuscripts and homiletical materials, Edwards did occasionally, as was previously asserted, produce a full manuscript work for special

---

29. Wilson H. Kimnach, Introduction to "A Strong Rod Broken and Withered," in *Works of Jonathan Edwards: Sermons and Discourses, 1743-1758*, ed. Wilson H. Kimnach (New Haven, CT: Yale University Press, 2006), 25:312-13.

30. Kimnach, "General Introduction," 10:91.

occasions.³¹ This fact does not validate Edwards's lack of development in preaching. As years of experience compile, moving to a semi-manuscript or a skeletal outline later in a minister's life is often a natural occurrence.³² Edwards was no different in this fashion, and possibly had mastered the pulpit in the category of extempore. However, he was still experimenting with new approaches to his notes, although the main headings remained the same.³³

Time was another factor of which Edwards had the reality of facing. In his early preaching, the manuscript gave him a guide to the length of time a sermon would consume. However, following twenty years of experience, by the mid-1740s, he was now experienced enough to discern the timeframe of a manuscript, semi-manuscript, or a skeletal outline. These are matters of discernment in relation to delivery that come strictly with experience, regardless of the century one preaches. Edwards was well on his way to achieving his maturation level but more hurdles were over the horizon.

### NORTHAMPTON SERMON FROM JUNE 1745

This is an additional sermon that was observed in its original form, titled "What I Intend at this Time to Shew [Is] what we are Taught Concerning Christ by These Names by Which He Is . . . Called." The sermon is from the text, *"And from Jesus Christ,* who is the faithful witness,

---

31. Wilson H. Kimnach, Preface to "The Period, 1743-1758," *Works of Jonathan Edwards: Sermons and Discourses, 1743-1758*, ed. Wilson H. Kimnach (New Haven, CT: Yale University Press, 2006), 25:313-14.

32. Through the preaching departments, many seminaries require students to prepare a manuscript sermon and an outline of the manuscript. Over twenty-six years of experience in preaching, the writer has developed sermon skills using a semi-manuscript form and a skeletal outline form. Many colleagues in ministry, who began preaching in the twentieth-century and have now moved into the twenty-first century, have also developed a shorter, more efficient usage of sermon notes.

33. The headings are those previously mentioned: Text, Doctrine, and Application.

and the first begotten of the dead, and the prince of the kings of the earth. Unto him that loved us, and washed us from our sins in his own blood" (Rev 1:5, KJV). This was a five-part sermon, and this first section from Revelation 1:5 (a), *"And from Jesus Christ,"* has some interesting characteristics in the original sermon.[34]

The first noticeable item is the handwriting enlargement where Edwards spells out "JESUS CHRIST," in large cursive letters following the writing of Revelation 1:5. The writing is reminiscent of a 1720s manuscript. Further, the Roman numeral I is enlarged, along with the word "JESUS" in the title. In addition, the paper used for this sermon has some interesting markings. Apparently, at one time, the front page of this sermon was used for personal correspondence. Evidently, part of Edwards's handwriting is upside down, and says, "If you have an opportunity of sending this by some Northampton man, this you see your.... I reviewed the last week's paper but those of the preceding two weeks, I missed, I desire you to send em."[35] This is another example of Edwards's frugality in using any type of paper he could salvage for sermon use.

Pages five-to-eight are from different paper as well, and are similar to the thin fan-like paper used in the "Farewell Sermon" of 1750.[36] On paper, Roman numeral II is similar to "Sinners" on pages nine-to-ten,

---

34. Jonathan Edwards, "What I Intend at this Time to Shew [Is] What We Are Taught Concerning Christ by These Names by Which He Is . . . Called (Rev. 1:5(a)." Edwards Collection, MSS 151, Box 14, Folder 1139 (New Haven, CT: Yale University, Beinecke Library, June 1745). The writer observed this sermon at the Beinecke Library, Yale University, September of 2009.

35. Ibid.

36. Kimnach, "General Introduction," 10:68. Kimnach says, "the fan paper is referred to by Dwight (*Life*, 487) as a by-product of the Edwards ladies' domestic industry, undertaken at Stockbridge to relieve the family of the heavy expenses of moving. . . . Dwight's testimony notwithstanding, fan papers appear in sermon manuscripts as early as 1745." Further, using notes from other occasions during the "1740s, in particular, Edwards used the blank versos of the 'bidden prayer' which was a 'written request for a congregational prayer, in making sermon booklets'."

and page ten is another upside-down text from a personal letter. Pages eleven-to-fourteen are written on the fine paper, clearly distinguishable from the other type.

Following the reference to Luke 2:10-11, two horizontal lines are underneath the Scripture texts, like in other sermons, as if Edwards is stressing to himself to read the entire text. On page fifteen, sermon notes are present, but on page sixteen, the final page, there are upside down notes also, seemingly from a different sermon. Once again, all of the sermon pages are sewn together with a single thread, woven in the middle of the pages in a vertical position. The dimensions of this duodecimo sermon are 4.25' X 4', and it has the characteristics of a semi-manuscript, one of Edwards's sermon approaches.[37]

Alexander B. Grosart described Edwards's sermons in terms of three classes. "In part fully written out, in larger part half-written out, and in largest part in simple notes."[38] "In part fully written out"[39] would describe the sermons in which Edwards recorded the thrust of his major thoughts without extensive elaboration. "In larger part half-written out"[40] would appear to be equivalent to the above "semi-manuscript Sermon."[41] "In largest part in simple notes,"[42] would be his description of the skeletal outline. The one category Grosart fails to mention is the fully written-out manuscript. Although full manuscripts were not as frequent during the last ten years at Northampton, Edwards did prepare them for special occasions.

---

37. Edwards, "What I Intend at this Time to Shew." The writer made observations of Edwards's sermon on Rev 1:5, at the Beinecke Library, Yale University, September of 2009.

38. Alexander B. Grosart, *Selections from the Unpublished Writings of Jonathan Edwards* (Ligonier, PA: Soli Deo Gloria Publications, 1992; originally printed by Rev. Alexander B. Grosart for private circulation, 1865), 11.

39. Ibid.
40. Ibid.
41. Ibid.
42. Ibid.

Grosart came to some conclusions during his research that all "three classes" of Edwards's manuscripts:

> shew, beyond all gainsaying, that his rule—in the proportion of 95 to 100—was to jot down the leading thoughts and illustrations, and trust to the suggestions of the moment for the recall of previous study, and meditation, and for the language. Let not, then, the great name of JONATHAN EDWARDS be adduced in support of the practice of invariably "reading" Sermons; a practice that, except in rare instances, quenches all real eloquence, breaks the spell of influence, unlooses the links of the electric chain that ought to bind a speaker and his audience and pass and repass thrills of feeling, and above all, leads to frauds of the most damaging and perilous sort.[43]

Grosart's assessment of Edwards's extemporaneous ability seems accurate, but he does fail to list the category of Edwards's occasional full manuscripts in the latter part of his Northampton years. Nevertheless, in Grosart's mind, little doubt existed about Edwards's preaching abilities. After reading the sermons, and travelling to America for a visit with Edwards's great-grandson, Rev. Tyron Edwards, Grosart was convinced. Furthermore, in the late 1740s, not only had Edwards developed in terms of the flexibility of his notes and delivery, the dynamics of his relationship to his congregation and community were deteriorating rapidly. Northampton was not focused as much on his delivery, as they were focused on his content that was out of harmony with his late grandfather, Solomon Stoddard.

## Northampton's Fear of Edwards's Persuasive Preaching

The Rev. Samuel Hopkins knew it was not Edwards's method of preaching that Northampton did not like; rather, it was his departure from Stoddard. Hopkins wrote about Edwards's preaching abilities in glowing terms:

---

43. Ibid., 14.

> Mr. Edwards had the most universal character of a good preacher of almost any minister in this age. There were but few that heard him, who did not call him a good preacher, however they might dislike his religious principles, and be much offended at the same truths when delivered by others; and most admired him above all that ever they heard.[44]

This was one of the personal evaluations affirming Jonathan Edwards's homiletical ability. Corporately, in 1750, Edwards's opponents refused to allow him to preach in order to defend his controversial communion views. Kimnach believes their reluctance communicates a fear of Edwards's power through preaching:

> In early 1749 he made a formal acknowledgement of his feelings before the committee of the church and asked for permission to preach in explanation of his position. Although a few members supported his proposal, the majority were opposed, and after some deliberation the committee instructed Edwards to publish his argument through the press. Curiously, they were willing to have a sensitive internal dispute aired before the world rather than risk Edwards' preaching to the church. There have been many tributes to the power of Edwards' preaching, but few stronger attestations than this, and none more from more expert authorities. Moreover, according to the detailed record of Edwards' "Narrative," the church rejected his half-dozen additional requests to preach on the subject during the remainder of 1749, and in 1750 the committee officially opposed his preaching the lecture series, though Edwards finally insisted upon his duty to speak, at least in the lecture venue, to those who would listen.[45]

---

44. Hopkins, *Life and Character*, 50.
45. Wilson H. Kimnach, Introduction to "Lectures on the Qualifications for Full Communion in the Church of Christ," in *Works of Jonathan Edwards: Sermons and Discourses, 1743-1758*, ed. Wilson H. Kimnach (New Haven, CT: Yale University Press, 2006), 25:349.

Although preaching his views on the communion controversy would not be an option, lecturing was permitted, prompting him to write "Lectures on the Qualifications for Full Communion in the Church of Christ." His text was, "Thus saith the Lord; No stranger, uncircumcised in heart, nor uncircumcised in flesh, shall enter into my sanctuary, of any stranger that is among the children of Israel" (Ezek 44:9, KJV). Edwards taught that this text could be applied to the New Testament Church, and this text here, as in other places in the Bible, is referring to "circumcision of heart" as equal to "conversion of heart and not moral sincerity." Further, he explains that "to be uncircumcised in heart is evidently the same as to be unconverted."[46]

Furthermore, those who are converted will show the visible signs of being a saint, and these are the ones who should be "admitted to the communion of the Christian church" as "visible saints."[47] The "visible saints," according to Edwards, are not "natural men," and the "visible saints" persevere in the faith and "hold long, and such religion of natural men is like seed in stony places that has got no root and therefore can't last, but presently withers away."[48] This was a lasting theme in Edwards's preaching, as he observed the faith of many people from the revivals "wither away." Some of the young people and older people had shown promising signs of conversion and were brought into the membership of the church, but after time had passed, many of these "had backslid."[49]

---

46. Jonathan Edwards, "Qualifications for Full Communion," in *Works of Jonathan Edwards: Sermons and Discourses, 1743-1758*, ed. Wilson H. Kimnach (New Haven, CT: Yale University Press, 2006), 25:354-55.

47. Ibid., 357.

48. Ibid., 369.

49. Gura, *Jonathan Edwards*, 138-39. Gura points out that some of the young people, like "Ebenezer Pomeroy, and Noah Baker" were involved in the bad book scandal, and "the controversy started predictably enough when the young men, all converts in Edwards's recent awakenings, began to lend the proscribed texts to one another for private reading and then to meet in small groups to make 'sport of what they read in the book'."

Additionally, Edwards followed suit with an apology from the Old and New Testaments with answers to his opponents' objections. The parable of the ten virgins is interpreted as the "wise and the foolish," representing two sets of people, "true saints, and hypocrites."[50] About the parable of the "Marriage Feast" (Matt 22:1-12), Edwards says, "The point we are upon is clearly demonstrated by this parable."[51] In arguing his position, he uses an example of those invited into the church as "both good and bad, are invited to come to Christ." His point is that the only way these are invited in is through Christ. Using imagery, as he often does, he says, "If a king should invite a whole city to come to an entertainment in his palace to feast with him, it won't follow that any one man is warranted by that to come there naked!"[52] The "unwarrantable" aspect of this story to Edwards was not only that he did not have a wedding garment, "but for coming in there without one."[53]

In his final statements, perhaps his most convincing argument to his opponents is in these words: "If ordinances are means of grace no otherwise than as a means of beginning grace, this would prove too much. That would prove that godly men must never attend 'em, for they don't attend 'em as a means of beginning grace, because grace is begun in them already."[54] In other words, what is the point in godly men continuing with the Lord's Supper if it is a means of beginning grace? Naturally, to Edwards, this would be a mundane exercise with no meaning or purpose to those who partake. Edwards realized his Grandfather Stoddard's practice propagated a works-based

---

50. Edwards, "Qualifications for Full Communion," 25:379.
51. Ibid., 380.
52. Ibid., 381.
53. Ibid.
54. Ibid., 434.

system, and he certainly did not feel comfortable promoting such a doctrinal system.

Edwards had come to understand that the Lord's Supper was for those who were already converted as full members, and only they were permitted to participate. Only they could comprehend the full measure of the practice itself. This was a matter of the heart, and Edwards believed that only regeneration could change a sinner's heart. However, his view regarding how a person was regenerated was beginning to be questioned, and after Edwards's death, this was not the only aspect of his doctrinal system that the New Divines would reformulate.

As Winslow claims,

> On its merits, the Halfway Covenant was a dead issue; revived, it acquired a significance which had far more to do with fair governance than with the communion of saints. The church member of 1750 was a democrat, although as yet he did not know it; and a good many of the "Boys of 76" were already born.[55]

Interestingly, Marsden points out, "the vast majority of Edwards' family and supporters, it might be added, supported the Revolution."[56] One thing these "Boys of 76" and their fathers, who presently opposed Edwards, were not going to permit, was Jonathan Edwards preaching his "Qualifications for Full Communion" to the entire congregation in Northampton. As Kimnach cited, their refusal was "a tribute to the power of Edwards' preaching."[57] It is evident that homiletically, by 1750, they knew Edwards all too well. However, strikingly obvious from Edwards's perspective was that he knew them better.

---

55. Winslow, *Jonathan Edwards*, 225.
56. Marsden, *Jonathan Edwards*, 369.
57. Kimnach, Introduction to "Qualifications," 25:349.

## Conclusion to the Northampton Communion Controversy, 1750

Jonathan Edwards not only sought to preach and lecture his way through the communion controversy, he also endeavored to write his way through. The reappearance of his full manuscript for his "Farewell Sermon" does not, however, translate into his ongoing dependence on the manuscript. Due to the intensity of the months preceding his termination, he would have to use and apply his entire arsenal of communication, writing, and apologetic skills.

"An Humble Inquiry into the Rules of the Word of God Concerning the Qualifications Requisite to a Compleat Standing and Full Communion in the Visible Christian Church," was written and published in 1749. Edwards gave his explanation as to why he disagreed with Solomon Stoddard. Edwards revealed his respect for his grandfather, but claims that "I ought not to look on his principles as oracles, as though he could not miss it...if I should believe his principles, [only] because he advanced them, I should be guilty of making him an idol."[58]

The volatility of this issue was now becoming a public spectacle in New England.[59] Thomas Prince, John Webb, Thomas Foxcroft, and

---

58. Jonathan Edwards, Author's preface to "An Humble Inquiry into the Rules of the Word of God Concerning the Qualifications Requisite to a Compleat Standing and Full Communion in the Visible Christian Church," in *Works of Jonathan Edwards: Ecclesiastical Writings*, ed. David D. Hall (New Haven, CT: Yale University Press, 1994), 12:168.

59. Jonathan Edwards, Personal letters to The Reverend Thomas Foxcroft, 24 May 1749, in *Letters and Personal Writings, Personal Narrative*, ed. George S. Claghorn (New Haven CT: Yale University Press, 1998), 16:284. In this letter to Rev. Foxcroft, Edwards tells him, "This western part of New England is exceeding full of noise about this affair, and few are indifferent. Some of the minister's of Connecticut . . . appear strangely ready to entertain groundless surprises, and receive false reports and misrepresentations concerning me, which the country is very full of."

Mather Byles wrote and signed the preface of "An Humble Inquiry into the Rules of the Word of God Concerning the Qualifications Requisite to a Compleat Standing and Full Communion in the Visible Christian Church," in which they all four avoid taking a stand, and basically say that Edwards should be respected and his views should be regarded. However, they give testimony that the views of their Puritan forefathers in New England were of Edwards's persuasion. Nevertheless, they acknowledge the obvious fact that "some good and learned men have since gone into another way of thinking in this matter."[60] Jonathan Edwards's late grandfather, Solomon Stoddard, was one of these "learned men," and he was called by some the "pope" of the Connecticut valley. These four men all knew they were walking on thin ice, but Edwards was the one willing and bold enough to take the lead in testing its thickness.

In this twenty-first century, as one reads the vast knowledge in Edwards's sermons, it is beyond comprehension to imagine Edwards leaving the ministry for some secular vocation. However, in his letter to Foxcroft, Edwards was apparently feeling so rejected that he thought about the potential of this ruining his ministerial occupation:

> If I should be wholly cast out of the ministry, I should be in many respects in a poor case. I shall not be likely to be serviceable to my generation, or get a subsistence in a business of a different nature. I am by nature very unfit for secular business; and especially am now unfit, after I have been so long in the work of the ministry. I am now comfortably settled, have as large a salary settled upon me as most have out of Boston, and have the largest and most

---

60. Thomas Prince, John Webb, Thomas Foxcroft, and Mather Byles, Preface to "An Humble Inquiry into the Rules of the Word of God Concerning the Qualifications Requisite to a Compleat Standing and Full Communion in the Visible Christian Church," in *Works of Jonathan Edwards: Ecclesiastical Writings*, ed. David D. Hall (New Haven, CT: Yale University Press, 1994), 12:172.

chargeable family of any minister, perhaps with an hundred miles of me...I seem as it were to be casting myself off from a precipice; and have no other way, but to go on, as it were blindfold, i.e. shutting my eyes to everything else but the evidences of the mind and will of God, and the path of duty; which I would observe with the utmost care.[61]

These words give evidence that Edwards felt as if the walls were closing in on him at Northampton and throughout the country. He had arrived at an ecclesiological position that he thought could bring change and reform for the spiritual health of the church. Now, however, he found himself in a position where he was consistently not permitted to use the best weapon, his preaching.

The lecture that Edwards had conducted was attended by more people from outside the church than those that were within the church. Two deacons, Noah Cook and Ebenezer Pomeroy, worked behind the scenes to undermine Edwards's efforts.[62] They both had listened to Edwards preach for many years, and they knew he had a way with words. Winslow said, "Like Emerson, Jonathan Edwards gave the impression of speaking from the immediate inspiration of the moment, in spite of the manuscript before him."[63]

However, the tide was rising against Edwards, and only a handful of the ministers on the council voted in his favor. Edward Billing was one whose support of Edwards during the controversy resulted in his termination also. Edwards could say nothing to turn the tide, and he knew it. In a letter to John Erskine on July 5, 1750, Edwards gave record of the vote:

When the church was convened in order to the council's knowing their minds with respect to my continuance, about

---

61. Edwards, Personal letter to Foxcroft, 16:284.
62. Patricia J. Tracy, *Jonathan Edwards Pastor: Religion and Society in Eighteenth Century Northampton* (New York: Hill and Wang, 1979), 177. Tracy mentions Ebenezer Pomeroy as being "the manager of the anti-Edwards crusade in Northampton."
63. Winslow, *Jonathan Edwards*, 129.

twenty-three appeared for it; others stayed away, choosing not to act either way. But the generality of the church, which consists of about 230 male members, voted for my dismission. My dismission was carried in the council by a majority vote of one vote. . . . The ministers were equally divided; but of the delegates one more were for it than against it. And so it happened that every member of the council that were of the churches of the people's choosing voted for my dismission, but every one that were of the churches that I chose were against it.[64]

Edwards's testimony indicates that a concerted effort was made on behalf of his opponents to force the odds against him. Further, Edwards pointed out that even some of his relatives, his cousin, "Joseph Hawley Jr. a man of lax principles in religion, falling in on some essential things with Arminians, and is very open and bold in it…was their chief spokesman."[65] Edwards describes Joseph Hawley Jr. as a "young gentleman of liberal education and notable abilities and a fluent speaker the age of about seven or eight and twenty years of age."[66] As Tracy claims, it is improbable that Hawley simply "seized his chance to begin his illustrious career as a popular political leader by adding his educated voice to the general outcry."[67]

Edwards's letters tell a different story that involves deeper issues. Twenty-three years earlier, Edwards had come to Northampton as a probationer, when Joseph Hawley Jr. was four years old, and now his ministry had come to an end. Edwards lamented, "I desire that such a time of awful changes, dark clouds, and great frowns of heaven on me

---

64. Jonathan Edwards, Personal letter to Rev. John Erskine, 5 July 1750, in *Works of Jonathan Edwards: Letters and Personal Writings, Personal Narrative*, vol. 16, ed. George S. Claghorn (New Haven, CT: Yale University Press, 1998), 16:353.
65. Ibid.
66. Ibid.
67. Tracy, *Jonathan Edwards Pastor*, 185.

and my people may be a time of serious consideration, thorough self-reflection and examination, and deep humiliation with me."[68]

Could anything else in Edwards's preaching have been underlying the issue of communion, or contributed to Edwards's dismissal? In other words, was another doctrine at the heart of the problem, but which could not be used to gain enough support for his dismissal? Edwards's words to Erskine certainly seem to assert this fact.

> I desire your fervent prayers for me and those who have heretofore been my people. I know not what will become of them. There seems to be the utmost danger that the younger generations will be carried away with Arminianism, as with a flood. The young gentleman [Hawley] I before spoke of is high in their esteem, and is become the most leading man in the town; and is very bold in declaring and disputing for his opinions; and we have none able to confront and withstand him in dispute: and some of the young people already show a disposition to fall in with his notions. And 'tis not likely that the people will obtain any young gentleman of the Calvinistical persuasion to settle with them in the ministry that will have courage and ability to make head against him. And as to the older people, there never appeared so great an indifference among them about things of this nature. They will at present be much more likely to be thorough in their care to settle a minister of principles contrary to mine, as to terms of communion, than to settle one that is sound in the doctrines of grace.[69]

Additionally, this Calvinistic controversy in Northampton was prominent in Edwards's mind prior to his dismissal, because he also told Erskine that, due to the communion controversy, he had to delay his "writing

---

68. Edwards, Personal letter to Rev. John Erskine, 16:354.
69. Ibid.

against Arminianism" after being "rent off from it by these difficulties."[70] Nevertheless, Edwards was not to be deterred in his ambition. During the year of 1753, in the midst of more difficulties in Stockbridge, Edwards would pen "The Freedom of the Will," and those who desired a copy could order by subscription beginning October 17, 1754.[71]

Edwards methodically dismantled each Arminian argument, and Winslow describes his strategy as, "With pitiless accuracy he finds the weak places in the enemy's armor, mows down objections, holds the opposing view up to scorn and defiance labeling it as 'absurd, impertinent,' and sometimes so 'nonsensical' as hardly to merit reply."[72] At the time Edwards penned his letter to the Reverend John Erskine on July 5, 1750, he had recently preached his Farewell Sermon to his congregation, and "The Freedom of the Will" was seminal in his mind. However, his future destination was unclear as he opened his heart and said, "But I am now as it were thrown upon the wide ocean of the world, and know not what will become of me and my numerous and chargeable family; nor have I any particular door in view, that I depend upon to be opened for my future serviceableness."[73]

Although Edwards had mastered much homiletically over the years with the Northampton congregation and had advanced his extemporaneous preaching as his Grandfather Stoddard had taught, his disagreement with Stoddard's ecclesiology and his increasingly unpopular Calvinistic views caused almost the entire town to loathe his preaching and to try and erase him—not only from the town itself, but even from their memories. In a 1754 letter to Joseph Hawley Jr., Edwards recalled the town's attitude toward him, "So deep were their prejudices, that their heat was maintained; nothing would quiet 'em till they could

---

70. Ibid., 355.
71. Winslow, *Jonathan Edwards*, 274.
72. Ibid., 277.
73. Edwards, Personal letter to Rev. John Erskine, 16:355.

see the town clear of root and branch, name and remnant."[74]

During this crucial period before his termination, Edwards appears to have reverted back to bulking his lectures, writing defenses and sermons with page-after-page of materials. His "Farewell Sermon," however, should not be used as evidence to prove that Edwards continued to rely on manuscripts at this point in his ministry. He obviously wanted to be thorough in leaving posterity these written documents, although his ability in presenting the sermon at this point far exceeded that of his days in New York City. He had transitioned well in the 1740s throughout this fourth stage, and his "Farewell Sermon" would mark the end of things as he knew them in Northampton, but also marked the beginning of a coming new stage for which he had very little experience.

## The Northampton "Farewell Sermon," July 1, 1750

With his dismissal now becoming a reality, Edwards would be given an opportunity to address the congregation with a "Farewell Sermon." This sermon has the characteristics of his important late 1740's manuscripts that are fully written out. Kimnach called this sermon:
> one of Edwards' most carefully crafted statements and a masterpiece among his sermons...and perhaps most notable is that, unlike virtually all his other sermon manuscripts, this sermon is given a formal title. Across the top of the first page of the manuscript in a relatively clear and large hand Edwards wrote: "My Farewell Sermon to the People of Northampton. Preached July 1, 1750."[75]

---

74. Edwards, Personal letter to Joseph Hawley Jr., 18 November 1754, in Jonathan Edwards, *Works of Jonathan Edwards: Letters and Personal Writings, Personal Narrative*, ed. George S. Claghorn (New Haven, CT: Yale University Press, 1998), 16:648.

75. Kimnach, "Watchman for Souls," 25:457.

He used the text, "As also ye have acknowledged us in part, that we are your rejoicing, even as ye also are ours, in the day of the Lord Jesus" (2 Cor 1:14, KJV).

An observation of the sermon in the manuscript form reveals some of Edwards's common abbreviations. He uses the circle with the dot in the middle for the word "world." For the words "Christ" and "Christian duty," he uses the X. On page twenty-nine of the forty-two-leaf sermon, the name of Job Strong is written rather large, next to the date of July 21, 1748, but Edwards marked a horizontal line through his name. On pages twenty-eight-to-thirty-one, a vertical line was drawn down the middle of the page, and the size of the leaf notes is duodecimo 4' X 3.75'. Additionally, Edwards used the curved horizontal lines in the particular divisions, much like in the 1741 "Sinners" sermon.

Toward the middle section of the sermon, the pages are cut in a curved shape made of a much finer material. Kimnach describes these as "scraps of rice paper left over from the family fan manufacture."[76] In addition, the sermon's physical characteristics could reveal possible evidence of the sermon being composed in stages. Edwards certainly had sufficient time to contemplate the "Farewell Sermon," while waiting on the verdict of the council and the people's vote.[77] Then, the verdict was in, and Edwards was out.

On July 1, 1750, when Edwards stood to preach this sermon, he must have felt the same inwardly as he did when preaching his first sermon as a probationer with Stoddard. He was as human as any man, and must have had mixed emotions on that July day while facing so many he believed betrayed the truth in exchange for the opinions

---

76. Ibid., 460.
77. Jonathan Edwards, "My Farewell Sermon to the People of Northampton (II Cor. 1:14)," Jonathan Edwards Collection, MSS 151, Box 14, Folder 1107 (New Haven, CT: Yale University, Beinecke Library, July 1, 1750). The writer made these observations on a visit to the Beinecke Library, Yale University, September of 2009.

of man. Reflecting today upon this turn of events, one could easily envision Edwards reverting homiletically back to his beginning days in New York, leaning heavily on his manuscript in order to communicate precisely what he wanted them to hear. However, from his vast experience, he certainly possessed the ability to preach this sermon predominantly memoriter. Perhaps his drafting of the manuscript was with the intention to leave his words for the sake of posterity.

Further, Edwards knew a handful of people with friendly expressions on their faces would be present, at least twenty-three men and their households, but they would be like speckles of salt on a large dark table compared to the two hundred and thirty against him. However, duty called once more, and perhaps Edwards remembered the words of the Lord to Jeremiah, the weeping prophet, "Be not afraid of their faces: for I am with thee to deliver thee, saith the Lord" (Jer 1:8, KJV).

From the beginning of this sermon, Edwards desires his audience to remember one theme, and that is although they may be separated in this world, "there is one meeting more that they must have, and that is in the last great day of accounts."[78] Edwards envisions a day when groups of people from the spiritual realm on earth will be gathered together by God to be judged according to their actions to God, their ministers, and to others. According to Edwards, the meeting will take place in an "unchangeable state," and now people live in a "mutable state."[79] Now is the time that affords people the opportunity to bring "happy changes" in their lives, but if they wait too long, in the "unchangeable state," it will be too late to change, "let him who is filthy, be filthy still" (Rev 22:11).[80]

---

78. Jonathan Edwards, "A Farewell Sermon Preached at the First Precinct in Northampton, After the People's Public Rejection of Their Minister on June 22, 1750," in *Works of Jonathan Edwards: Sermons and Discourses, 1743-1758*, ed. Wilson H. Kimnach (New Haven, CT: Jonathan Edwards Center at Yale University, 1992), 25:463.

79. Ibid., 465.

80. Ibid., 466.

Further, Edwards points out that they will "meet together in a state of clear, certain, and infallible light." This includes, "Christ will be made known; and there shall no longer be any debate, or difference of opinions; the evidence of the truth shall appear beyond all dispute, and all controversies shall be finally and forever decided."[81] Additionally, ministers and people will come to know who has been "faithful," and who has not. The "judge will not only declare justice, but will do justice between ministers and their people."[82]

Naturally, Edwards mentions things indirectly that are meant to be associated with the previous "communion controversy." He then follows by quoting a verse that he seems to apply to himself, "And whosoever shall not receive you, nor hear your words, when ye depart out of that house or city, shake off the dust off your feet" (Matt 10:14-15). Furthermore, ministers are not only sent by God to do a work for him, they will return to him to give an account to him.[83]

In the application section, Edwards reminds them he served as their minister "three and twenty years, the 15th day of last February."[84] He tells them he labored to give them God's Word all these years, and follows by asserting that they will have to "give an account" for the "improvement" in their lives from his "ministry."[85] He describes this Day of Judgment as a time when "our hearts will 'be turned inside out', and the secrets of them will be made more plainly to appear than our outward actions do now."[86] Further, Edwards was concerned about those who had sat under his ministry for many years, but had never come to true conversion. He says their parting causes him to be melancholy, because "I leave you in the gall of bitterness and bond of

---

81. Ibid., 467.
82. Ibid., 470.
83. Ibid., 473.
84. Ibid., 475.
85. Ibid., 475-76.
86. Ibid., 476.

iniquity, having the wrath of God abiding on you, and remaining under condemnation to everlasting misery and destruction."[87]

Regarding the youth, he alludes to the bad-book scandal saying, "I formerly led this church to some measure, for the suppressing vice among our young people, which gave so great offense, and by which I became so obnoxious. I have sought the good and not the hurt of our young people."[88] Regarding the children, he urges them to "constantly pray," and regarding the "Christian family," he urges "to be as it were a little church, consecrated to Christ, and wholly influenced and governed by his rules."[89]

The final two groups he challenges are the "contentious people" and those who were his supporters in the "late controversy." He gives the "contentious" a tongue lashing, by claiming that since he first became their pastor, they were "one of the greatest burdens" he had had to contend with over his years of ministry. Their contentions were not just with the minister; rather they also were "with one another, about your lands, and other concerns."[90] During the times of revival, during 1734-35 and 1740-42, one of the attributes of the awakening that excited Edwards was the subsiding of these "contentions." However, in his "Farewell Sermon," he makes it clear that for the greater part of his ministry, these "contentious people" caused him and others great heartache.

The final words to the congregation affirm the words of Edwards's July 5, 1750, letter to the Reverend John Erskine regarding the prevailing movement toward Arminian ideas. Edwards tells the congregation, "Another thing that vastly concerns the future prosperity of the town, is that you should watch against the encroachments of error; and

---

87. Ibid., 479.
88. Ibid., 482.
89. Ibid., 484.
90. Ibid., 485.

particularly Arminianism, and doctrines of like tendency."[91] Edwards had sensed in the previous "seven years," a rapid movement among the younger people away from Calvinistic orthodoxy. He told the congregation that these "corrupt principles...are still prevailing and creeping into almost all parts of the land, threatening the utter ruin of the credit of those doctrines, which are the peculiar glory of the gospel, and the interests of vital piety."[92] Edwards firmly believed and preached that, if these Arminian doctrines prevailed, "It will threaten the spiritual and eternal ruin of this people, in the present and future generations."[93]

In closing, Edwards's concern for them acquiring a godly minister is both moving and powerful:

> If you should happen to settle a minister, who knows nothing truly of Christ, and the way to salvation by him, nothing experimentally of the nature of vital religion; alas, how will you be exposed as sheep without a shepherd! Here is need of one in this place, who shall be eminently fit to stand in the gap, and make up the hedge, and who shall be as the chariots of Israel, and the horsemen thereof. You need one that shall stand as a champion in the cause of truth and the power of godliness.... And let us all remember, and never forget our future solemn meeting, on that great day of the Lord; the day of infallible decision, and of the everlasting and unalterable sentence, Amen.[94]

Stunningly, this would not be Edwards's last amen in the Northampton Church. Hopkins later recorded that Edwards occasionally supplied the pulpit when no one else was available. However, after the committee in later months called for the opinion of the town, the

---

91. Ibid., 486.
92. Ibid.
93. Ibid.
94. Ibid., 488.

vote was unanimous that "he should not preach among them."[95]

As Edwards was traveling more to preach out of town following his dismissal, previously they invited him to preach upon his return. However, the fear once again regarding the strength of Edwards's preaching became evident, as they stopped inviting him altogether. On those Sundays, in the absence of a supply preacher, the congregation chose rather to worship among themselves.[96]

Seemingly, the most important days of Edwards's preaching career were over. However, the Lord had one more pastoral stop for Edwards's earthly pilgrimage. Stockbridge, on the western frontier, would be his new home from 1751 until the beginning of 1758. He would be tested in more ways than one, and his preaching would face yet another test, preaching to two congregations that spoke different languages. Now his mastery of his first four stages with the manuscripts, semi-manuscripts, skeletal outlines, and extemporaneous delivery would all be tested in various ways in which he had no experience whatsoever.

## Contemporary Application of Stage Four: Completing the Homiletical Stages with Extemporaneity

The skeletal outlines of Jonathan Edwards appear to reveal a new more advanced communication attempt on his part, even perhaps without an outline. Skeletal outlines do pose a challenge for many homileticians because of the absence of written information. All the way through the year 1750, and Edwards's Farewell Sermon, he continued occasionally to write a full manuscript for previously stated reasons. The presence of Edwards's abbreviated sermon outlines gives some credibility to his interest and use of the extemporaneous approach.

---

95. Hopkins, *Life and Character*, 68.
96. Ibid.

Skeletal outlines were discussed in the previous chapter, and they do pose challenges today because they require experience and often years of mastering the other sermon stages. To complete this segment of Edwards's stages of development, the continuous need to polish the homiletical delivery is crucial.

In order for the contemporary to preach without a skeletal outline or memoriter, as Edwards may have attempted, the writer believes one needs to be familiar with the following four elements. First, there needs to be a solid understanding of how the overall content of the sermon is linked together structurally in a coherent way. Second, there needs to be memorization of the main core of ideas in the Text, Doctrine, and Application sections of the sermon as discussed previously. Third, from a subjective standpoint, the homily should stem from the heart so as to communicate greater pathos to the recipients and an increase in eye contact throughout the sermon. Fourth, as Edwards had extemporaneous examples, possibly in his Grandfather Stoddard and George Whitefield, contemporaries need a mentor who is a model of extemporaneous ability, support, and constructive criticism.

One of the primary ways Edwards is a solid example of coherency is due to his eighteenth-century sermon structure remaining relevant with only a few minor changes. For example, in 1995, several professors at Southwestern Baptist Theological Seminary taught the following preaching structure: Introduction, Reading of the Text, Explanation of the Text under each main Roman numeral point, Illustrations along with each main point of the text, and Application of the text in contemporary times, and a smooth Transition Statement from point-to-point.[97] Similarly, Edwards used a triad of Text, Doctrine, and Application

---

97. While enrolled in the Master of Divinity with Biblical Languages (M.Div. BL.) degree at Southwestern Baptist Theological Seminary in Fort Worth, Texas, during the twentieth century, the writer learned this sermon structure from his preaching professor, Grant Lovejoy.

(Use), for his sermon structure. Consequently, in light of contemporary standards, the result is that Edwards's sermons have maintained strong structural relevance.[98]

A final important observation regarding this tri-section approach is the utility of an extemporaneous delivery. After mastering the manuscript stage, semi-manuscript, skeletal outline, and the sermon structure itself, preaching memoriter or preaching extemporaneously may follow without being forced. Delivering a homily in this fourth stage as Kroll defines,

> does not imply speaking without preparation. There is careful and detailed preparation, but it is not carried to the pulpit. The speaker prepares an outline which will trigger his thoughts remembering the preparation he has done in the study. It is to be distinguished from the impromptu method. In general conversation, the word extempore means without preparation, but never so with regard to speech. This name is given to this form of delivery because the speaker is so well versed in his material that it appears as if he is delivering his speech or sermon "off the cuff."[99]

If an individual is to be successful in achieving extemporaneous delivery, a conscious effort to make eye contact and think about nonverbal communication often referred to as "body language" is important. Robinson believes "eye contact probably ranks as the most effective single means of nonverbal communication" at the speaker's

---

98. Smith, *Dying to Preach*, 124-25. Numerous other approaches exist to preaching; however, Edwards's approach to Text, Doctrine, and Application finds precision. Smith makes a good argument about the possibility of losing precision in modern methods. He writes, "We must be precise. . . . The primary reason is that when we handle Scripture, the congregation generally believes that they are hearing what God has to say on a particular topic. The reason that people think God is so glaringly irrelevant could be because preachers have glossed over doctrinal truths in a way that makes them bland and unappealing."

99. Kroll, *Prescription for Preaching*, 118-19.

disposal.[100] If an individual never looks at the audience, it will make feedback difficult. With the eyes one can discern whether people are listening intently or losing interest. Additionally, eye contact with the audience helps the speaker and the audience make a better connection through the communication process. The realization of these facts should be another incentive to strive for homiletical excellence through mastery of the different stages. Edwards believed they were important, and Bailey estimates that Edwards "made an effort to connect with both the heart and intellect of his auditors."[101] Edwards believed in understanding his audience, and understood that his homiletical duty was to communicate clearly where they were on life's journey. Bryan Chapell, a well-respected writer on contemporary preaching, says,

> Thus, insights from the exegetical outline, the passage's background, and the present level of a congregation's knowledge about these matters must all funnel into a homiletical outline in order for a competent sermon to take shape. . . . An exegetical outline establishes what a text says. A homiletical outline establishes how a text's meaning is best communicated to a congregation.[102]

Edwards understood these concepts and also had several mentors he could look to regarding sermon structure, eye contact, and effective extemporaneous delivery. One came early in his ministry through his Grandfather Solomon Stoddard, and the second charismatic figure was George Whitefield. Although Stoddard was a commanding figure in his day, Whitefield possibly stunned Edwards with his booming voice and extemporaneous delivery. Deep down he probably knew he would never be as commanding and charismatic as these two men; however, these men had communication qualities that revealed to him a higher

---

100. Robinson, *Biblical Preaching*, 201.
101. Bailey, "Driven By Passion," 70.
102. Bryan Chapell, *Christ Centered Preaching: Redeeming the Expository Sermon*, 2nd ed. (Grand Rapids: Baker Academic, 2005), 116.

standard with the potential to bring out his best.

Contemporary communicators of the Word have the ability to listen, observe, and learn from mentors and others. Not only did Edwards learn through auditory at a young age, he also learned through observation as a middle-aged man. Many able expositors today have achieved extemporaneous abilities in preaching. John MacArthur is one who often preaches at conferences and conventions simply from his overflow of knowledge. Albert Mohler often preaches with the appearance of not using notes, and is brilliant at maintaining eye contact with the audience. With modern technological advances, exemplary figures such as these can be watched and listened to on a daily basis. However, choosing a person of quality may be more important than quantity of time. Jesus' disciples were limited in their time learning under Jesus, but they had the greatest teacher of all time. MacArthur says,

> These few men, whose backgrounds were in mundane trades and earthly occupations, had little more than eighteen months' training for the monumental task to which they were called. There was no second string, no backup players, no plan B if the Twelve should fail…the entirety of their training for the task took less than half as long as it typically takes to get a degree from a seminary today. But Christ knew what He was doing. From His divine perspective, the ultimate success of the strategy actually depended on the Holy Spirit working in those men to accomplish His sovereign will. It was a mission that could not be thwarted. That's why it was a work for which God alone deserves praise and glory. Those men were merely instruments in His hands just as you and I can be God's instruments today.[103]

---

103. John MacArthur, *Twelve Ordinary Men, How the Master Shaped His Disciples for Greatness, and What He Wants to Do with You* (Nashville: W Publishing Group, A Division of Thomas Nelson, 2002), Introduction, xv.

In conclusion, the extant manuscripts from Edwards's early preaching career imply at a young age he leaned heavily on the manuscript form. However, as discussed previously, Edwards's later development and use of the skeletal outlines is also present from his extant sermons. For modern students of Edwards, he went through five stages of sermon development while endeavoring to make his shift from reliance on the manuscript to a skeletal outline.

First, he had learned through auditory early in life and had established a seminal idea surrounding the foundation of the sermon form. Second, Edwards seemed to come to a realization as an inexperienced preacher of his need to write and master the manuscript form. In order to improve his delivery, Edwards discovered that the manuscript preaching event itself would bring a more experienced and refined homiletic. Third, with experience in writing the manuscript and delivering the content via the homily, he recognized, along with his congregation, that his communication had made a dramatic improvement and abbreviated forms appear. Through this maturity in the pulpit, and the aid of the Holy Spirit, he started to realize that his thoughts had begun to flow more frequently *ad libitum*; thus, he began writing only partial ideas (semi-manuscript and skeletal). Fourth, he also learned by observing other extemporaneous preachers (i.e., George Whitefield, in 1740), that effective, Spirit-filled extemporaneous preaching could be accomplished and effective with the sole use of a skeletal outline. Using the historical and written evidence from Edwards's development, twenty-first-century practitioners possess the opportunity to observe these stages and make personal progress.

Having discussed the first four stages, it is important also to note that Edwards developed this process over many years of experience. Furthermore, by studying and practicing his stages, individuals today may potentially expedite sermon improvement in a shorter time span than Edwards and improve the sermon form and delivery. In other words, if those who are seeking improvement will study and understand all of Edwards's stages of development, they can implement them personally and potentially accelerate maturity toward proficiency.

With a comfortable command of four, he had one more stage to conquer and several more tests on the horizon. For the aging Edwards, it would not be painless transitioning as the Pastor of two congregations with different languages and eventually accepting the call as a College President. He would have to lean on his vast experience by transitioning and adapting as a communicator of God's Word far beyond the dependence on manuscripts.

CHAPTER 5

# Jonathan Edwards's

## MULTIFACETED MATURATION AND TRANSITIONAL ABILITIES AS A MISSIONARY PREACHER AND A COLLEGE PRESIDENT

Some concede the fact that Jonathan Edwards had arrived at a mature level in his sermon form and development by the time he moved to Stockbridge, in 1751.[1] However, his new assignment forced him to learn a new fifth way of communicating the sermon form with which he was so familiar. On February 22, 1751, Edwards received his call to settle as minister in Stockbridge, and on August 8, 1751, the church formally installed him as pastor.[2]

---

1. Kimnach, "General Introduction," 10:122. Kimnach says, "Edwards had surely mastered the pulpit by 1735…and gained all the mastery he was ever to have over the sermon form by 1727."
2. Minkema, *Chronology*, 21-22.

On October 18, 1751, Edwards's family moved to Stockbridge from King Street, but it was not until February, of 1752, that the Edwards's house finally sold.[3] His family experienced financial hardships, and in a letter to his father in January, of 1752, Edwards told his father Timothy that he could not help his sister, because "I am at this time; who, by reason of lately marrying two children, and the charge of buying, building and removing, am, I suppose, about 2,000 pounds in debt, in this province's money."[4]

In Stockbridge, they would also have turmoil with the Williams family, deal with others' prejudices toward the Indians, and make adjustments to life on the western frontier.[5] In spite of all of these trials, Edwards continued to write another response in the communion controversy by completing his "Misrepresentations Corrected, and Truth Vindicated." Additionally, he wrote and published "Freedom of the Will," in 1754, and in May, of 1757, he completed "Original Sin."[6] Perhaps one of Jonathan Edwards's most amazing characteristics was his unending ability to cope with impending problems and yet continue to preach and produce monumental writings. This attribute is a testimony to his lifelong spiritual, mental, and intellectual disciplines.

## STOCKBRIDGE AND A NEW HOMILETIC

Having spoken years earlier to David Brainerd about missions among the Indians, and now experiencing it firsthand, Jonathan Edwards understood

---

3. Ibid.
4. Jonathan Edwards, Personal letter to Timothy Edwards, January 1752, in *Works of Jonathan Edwards: Letters and Personal Writings, Personal Narrative*, ed. George S. Claghorn (New Haven, CT: Yale University Press, 1998), 16:421.
5. Stephen J. Nichols, "Last of the Mohican Missionaries, Jonathan Edwards at Stockbridge," in *American Religion and the Evangelical Tradition: The Legacy of Jonathan Edwards*, ed. D. G. Hart, Sean Michael Lucas, and Stephen J. Nichols (Grand Rapids: Baker Book House, 2003), 48-49.
6. Minkema, *Chronology*, 26.

that he was in a unique preaching situation. In fact, he discovered very quickly that the Indian mission demanded "a new kind of preaching."[7]

Three characteristics stand out in the Stockbridge sermons from the earlier eras. First, Edwards used many narrative texts that contained simple stories he hoped would relate to the Indians' comprehension of the sermons.[8] Second, the sermons from the Stockbridge era are noticeably shorter—especially the ones preached to the Indian congregation, and Edwards also re-preached previous Northampton sermons to the English congregation. Third, because a large separation from the Indians existed in culture, background, and education, many in the Indian congregation did not have the biblical reference points needed for a more immediate understanding, making the precise communication of the message more difficult for Edwards.

An additional hurdle for Edwards was speaking through an interpreter.[9] A normal one-hour sermon could easily become a two-hour exchange between Edwards, the interpreter, whose name was John Wauwaumpequunnaunt, and the Indian recipients.[10] The brevity of his

---

7. Wilson H. Kimnach, "Preface to the Period," in *Works of Jonathan Edwards: Sermons and Discourses, 1743-1758*, ed. Wilson H. Kimnach (New Haven, CT: Yale University Press, 2006), 25:40.

8. Ibid., 46.

9. Rachel M. Wheeler, "Living Upon Hope: Mohicans and Missionaries, 1730-1760" (Ph.D. diss., Yale University, 1999), 198-99. Wheeler believes that "John Wauwaumpequunaut served for a number of years as Edwards' interpreter. Although Wauwaumpequunaut appears only infrequently in Edwards' correspondence, the tone of these mentions suggests an affection and respect for the man. The story of Wauwaumpequunaut's arrival in Stockbridge is told by John Sergeant in his diary. In 1740, the 17 year old John had left his family against their will to attend Timothy Woodbridge's school. He made good progress and was funded as one of the Hollis boys. When Sergeant asked the boy why he wanted to learn, Wauwaumpequunaut replied that he thought 'it might be a means of knowing God.' A dozen years later, the 30 year old Wauwaumpequunaut was serving as Edwards' interpreter and as usher for Woodbridge in his school."

10. Marsden, *Jonathan Edwards*, 392.

bare, skeletal outlines are literary witnesses to Edwards becoming a homiletical redactionary, in order to accommodate the Housatunnocks and the Mohicans. Nichols says, "Edwards' extant sermons from this period reveal his concern not to overshoot his audience. . . . Edwards demonstrates a remarkable ability within the Stockbridge sermons to communicate clearly and effectively."[11]

This disparity between Edwards and his audience is obvious and unavoidable, whether advertently or inadvertently. Winslow describes the situation in a seemingly droll way:

> Certainly to Jonathan Edwards there was nothing inconsistent about the picture of himself in the role these memoranda suggest. For a later day, like so many other pictures which might recall his story, this one is made of strangely incongruous elements: the log meetinghouse, a handful of grave-faced Indians sitting in straight rows, their blankets drawn close around them; behind the desk one of the great intellects of his time, in a quiet voice saying, It is not good to get drunk.[12]

However, to Edwards, the situation was more serious. He was set on fulfilling his calling and preaching to the best of his ability. His own handwriting recorded the "'profession of Faith' of two Stockbridge Indians, Corneilus and Mary Munniwaumimmich."[13]

Although plowing the fallow ground had been difficult, the Stockbridge seeds Edwards had planted were beginning to grow, and that was enough to encourage him to keep looking forward, with his "hand to the plough" (Luke 9:62, KJV). Regarding the conversion narratives, Wheeler said,

---

11. Nichols, *Last of the Mohican Missionaries*, 57. Additionally, Nichols points out that "the chief criticism is that because Edwards never learned the language, his work was of limited impact and importance. Examining the case a little further reveals, however, that such estimates are misguided."

12. Winslow, *Jonathan Edwards*, 262.

13. Josh Moody, *Jonathan Edwards and the Enlightenment: Knowing the Presence of God* (Lanham, MD: University Press of America, 1992), 30.

There is no evidence that Edwards required Indian applicants to the church to deliver a narrative of their conversion, though it is to be assumed that he did. Edwards' commitment to the practice had cost him his pulpit in Northampton. It would have been wholly out of character for Edwards to establish different admission standards for Indian congregants.[14]

This must have taken a great deal of patience on Jonathan Edwards's behalf. In her journal, Esther Burr said, "My honored Father . . . while of late years, writing on his abstract treatises, and preaching largely to the Indians of Stockbridge, who are but little demonstrative, he has grown more and more careless of outward grace."[15] In other words, the Indians were not a people who were concerned about "demonstrative" communication. With Edwards possibly having to preach at a snail's pace through an interpreter, his "outward" demonstrations during preaching were reduced, and communicating the Word effectively through an interpreter had become the priority. Additionally, one must understand that his daughter, Esther, had grown up in Northampton, witnessing her father preach in one of the most influential New England churches. Not only was she amazed by the change in her father's homiletical approach to the Indians, it is suggested that she preferred watching him preach in the Northampton mode.

### "HEAVEN'S DRAGNET": AN EARLY INDIAN SERMON

One of Edwards's early sermons was "Heaven's Dragnet," preached in January, of 1751, to the Stockbridge Indians, from the text, "Again, the kingdom of heaven is like unto a net" (Matt 13:47-50). The sermon is an

---

14. Wheeler, "Living upon Hope," 199.
15. Esther Burr, "January 1754 Entry," *Journal of Esther Burr*, ed. Jeremiah Eames Ranking, 79 [on-line]; accessed December 28, 2009; available at Books.google.com; Internet.

octavo booklet of only four leaves, and Edwards did not stitch the pages.[16] The content is simple, yet strikingly clear regarding the fishermen and their net. Edwards explains the text first, by explaining the kingdom of heaven being "like a net."[17] The "net," according to Edwards, does not catch every fish in the sea and, thus, the "kingdom of Christ don't take all the world, but only a part."[18] The sermon depicts Christ as "the fisherman," and those "peculiar" are the ones who "belong to the fisherman."[19]

In the doctrine section, he told them that the Disciples of Christ were truly "fishermen." Christ told them that "they should no longer catch fish," "but he would 'make 'em fishers of men, to catch men'."[20] These are hints that Edwards had not changed his views on church membership since leaving Northampton, and continued by saying, "So none ought to come into the Christian church but good men."[21] Further, he seemed to clarify his position from his recent experiences, whether it was intentional or not. "Because ministers can't know men's hearts, every sort will come in, good and bad. As there will be some bad fish in the net, so there will be some bad men in the kingdom of Christ."[22]

As the sermon progressed, Edwards introduced simplistic eschatological concepts regarding judgment in relation to the separation on the shore of the "mixed together . . . good or bad," fish and men.[23] In his own words, he described God as casting "away wicked men, and Christ at the end of the world: the angels shall come forth and sever the wicked from among

---

16. Jonathan Edwards, introduction to "Heaven's Dragnet," in *Works of Jonathan Edwards, Sermons and Discourses, 1743-1758*, ed. Wilson H. Kimnach (New Haven, CT: Yale University Press, 2006), 25:576.
17. Ibid., 577.
18. Ibid.
19. Ibid.
20. Ibid., 578.
21. Ibid.
22. Ibid.
23. Ibid.

the just."²⁴ He said that the end of these wicked will come when God kindles a fire and "casts [them] into a furnace of fire."²⁵

The closing of the application section seems to be an analogy directed at the Indians who are agrarian and familiar with hunting. Those who "used to eat and drink together, and used to go hunting together, shall be separated one from another, never to be together anymore."²⁶ The New Testament verse about "two grinding at the mill, one shall be taken, and the other left" (Matt 24:41), is quoted in the context of "parents being separated from their children." In the end, "the one shall go into everlasting life, the other into everlasting burnings . . . and the reason that some men reform their lives for a little while only, and then never again. Their hearts were never changed."²⁷ People with unchanged hearts will be "cast into the furnace of fire."²⁸

The sermon, "Heaven's Dragnet," seems to flow well and is short and to the point. Whether Edwards believed he had delivered it to their understanding stands in question. An entirely different dynamic is present when preaching through an interpreter, whether on a foreign or home mission field. Many of Edwards's sermonic practices with the Indians were through trial-and-error. Although he had prior knowledge of communicating to the Indians through Brainerd's experiences, preaching successfully himself was another matter. Winslow says, "he admitted willingly that for the teaching of 'savages' he had neither aptitude nor training."²⁹

Winslow openly criticized Edwards for not gaining proficiency in the Housatunnock and Mohawk languages. "His children, who heard more Indian than English, all spoke it fluently, but his own proficiency in

---

24. Ibid.
25. Ibid., 579.
26. Ibid., 580.
27. Ibid., 581.
28. Ibid.
29. Winslow, *Jonathan Edwards*, 247.

the tongues was reserved for ancient Hebrew."[30] To complicate matters even more, Edwards had the Williams family to contend with again in Stockbridge. He preached about "Heaven's Dragnet," but Winslow speaks of a different kind of net, "a veritable net, spread by the same enemies he was leaving behind," supposedly in Northampton.[31]

## DANGERS ON THE FRONTIER: "IN THE NAME OF THE LORD OF HOSTS"—1754 TO 1755

During Edwards's time at Stockbridge, his family and the other settlers also faced impending dangers from Indian attacks and loss of the life of Col. Ephraim Williams Jr., near Crown Point. In 1755, the Edwards family had to fortify their home against the threat of an Indian attack.[32] Later in 1755, they were facing the reality of the coming Seven Years War, additionally termed the French and Indian War (1756-1763).

During these years, Edwards preached sermons regarding the conflict of war, such as, "In the Name of the Lord of Hosts."[33] His text on this occasion was:

> Then David said to the Philistine, "Thou comest to me with a sword, and with a spear, and with a shield: but I come unto thee in the name of the Lord of hosts. . . . This day will the Lord deliver thee into mine hand; and I will smite thee, and take thine head from thee; . . . for the battle is the Lord's, and he will give you into our hands" (1 Sam 17:45-47).

---

30. Ibid., 261.
31. Ibid., 247.
32. Murray, *Jonathan Edwards*, 389.
33. Jonathan Edwards, "In the Name of the Lord of Hosts," *Works of Jonathan Edwards: Sermons and Discourses, 1743-1758*, ed. Wilson H. Kimnach (New Haven, CT: Yale University Press, 2006), 25:682.

Edwards's note at the top of the first of six leaves says, "St[ockbridge] Ind[ians] on Occasion of the Expedition to Cr[own] Point & c. July 55."³⁴ The sermon is highly theological, and he warns them, "Men that trust in themselves make gods of themselves...man [is] but a worm."³⁵ Being able to justify going to war involves God allowing "us to go [to] war, and calls us to it in [his] providence... and Christ is willing to be a captain to them that choose him. He looks on their armies as his armies.... This is the way because God is a just and righteous God."³⁶

He says that the enemy (French) would make them "miserable," and depicts the enemy as a "Goliath" and "very proud."³⁷ Additionally, he vehemently attacks

> the religion of the Papists, that they are of, is contrary to God's word, and what he hates. The Pope [is an impostor; Papists] pray to images, and pray to [the] Virgin Mary. [They] pray to dead men. [The] Pope contrived for his people to get away money from the people [by selling them] pardon [for] sin. [They] pretend that in another world there is a fire that is on this side hell, where their people lie a great while,...[They] won't let the people have the Bible.³⁸

He concludes by urging them to "put away all sin," and assuring them that with God on their side, they will be "happy."³⁹ Edwards began the sermon by urging them not to "trust in themselves" and, in his final thoughts, he reminds them that "He is strong."⁴⁰

---

34. Wilson H. Kimnach, Introduction to "In the Name of the Lord of Hosts," in *Works of Jonathan Edwards: Sermons and Discourses, 1743-1758*, ed. Wilson H. Kimnach (New Haven, CT: Yale University Press, 2006), 25:681.
35. Edwards, "Lord of Hosts," 25:682.
36. Ibid., 682-83.
37. Ibid., 683.
38. Ibid.
39. Ibid., 684.
40. Ibid.

## Edwards's Visit to Hadley—October 1756

Although Edwards moved to Stockbridge in 1751, he travelled and preached in various places, including Hadley, Massachusetts. Today, as people travel out of Northampton, Massachusetts, and drive over the Connecticut River below, they can imagine George Whitefield ferrying across the river on October 17, 1740, after preaching at Hadley that morning.[41] However, sixteen years later, in 1756, Jonathan Edwards was the one ferrying across the Connecticut to preach at Hadley for a young man named Samuel Hopkins Jr. Kimnach describes him by saying, "He was the son of Samuel and Esther Edwards Hopkins of West Springfield, Massachusetts, thus Edwards' nephew."[42] However, "this Samuel Hopkins was no Edwardsean; indeed, he was a professed Stoddardean who believed that communion was a 'converting ordinance' and thus should be open, and he also looked favorably upon the halfway covenant."[43]

With these differences, and Edwards's past in nearby Northampton, it is perplexing to think about why Hopkins invited him to preach.[44] The answer may never be known. However, the sermon is typical of Edwards in some ways, and Kimnach calls it "a homiletical paradox."[45] Nevertheless, the sermon is not as complex as some make it out to be, but

---

41. Marsden, *Jonathan Edwards*, 206.

42. Samuel Hopkins, who was married to Esther Edwards, also is known as Samuel Hopkins ("the elder"). His son, Samuel Hopkins Jr., was the pastor at Hadley, Massachusetts. Samuel Hopkins ("the younger"), who studied under Jonathan Edwards, was the nephew of Samuel Hopkins ("the elder").

43. Wilson H. Kimnach, Introduction to "Of Those Who Walk in the Light of God's Countenance," in *Works of Jonathan Edwards: Sermons and Discourses, 1743-1758* (New Haven, CT: Yale University Press, 2006), 25:698.

44. Ibid. Regarding this preaching event, Kimnach asks, "Just what compound of familial affection and ecclesiastical diplomacy would have induced the Rev. Mr. Hopkins to invite his uncle to preach to his people, or for his uncle to accept the invitation, remains a matter for speculation, since there seems to be no extant documentation of the episode beyond Edwards' cryptic note on the sermon manuscript."

45. Ibid.

one might find subtle references to Edwards's church membership views hidden within the sermon content. Kimnach perhaps overlooks several of these facts. In his introduction to the sermon, he compares the message to a "modern formal structure" that "Edwards was increasing by using—but which had been introduced by liberal preachers—with an attempt to define the life of the elect in romantic, experiential terms reminiscent of Edwards' earlier preaching."[46] His most accurate assessment is regarding the sermon being "reminiscent" of Edwards's earlier preaching—perhaps in New York or in Bolton, Connecticut.

However, this sermon is another example of Edwards always being aware of the dynamics surrounding his audience. When he preached to preachers in Boston, he knew how to approach his audience. During the awakenings, Edwards preached to each audience, having possibly premeditated the entire scene before the sermon delivery. Furthermore, he approached his audiences in Stockbridge with the same scrutiny, and a solo performance like this one in Hadley was probably no different. In fact, his close proximity to Hadley for twenty-three years, while in Northampton, and prior knowledge of his nephew's views, gave him a great advantage as to his sermonic approach on his visit to Hadley. He may have changed his message structurally and "methodologically," but he did not compromise the strength and consistency of his content. This event is yet another example of Edwards adapting and transitioning in short periods of time from one type of audience to another.

## Hadley: "The Light of God's Countenance"—October 1756

Observing the historical chronology of Edwards's life in Stockbridge, one discovers that he traveled quite frequently to other places to preach

---

46. Ibid., 698-99.

and visit friends and family. By horseback, Stockbridge to Hadley was approximately forty to forty-five miles through the country. However, the Edwards family was no stranger to traveling great distances throughout Massachusetts and Connecticut, in order to visit their acquaintances in Boston, Windsor Farms, and New Haven.[47] With the pressures of life and ministry in Stockbridge, a ride to preach somewhere else for a week was probably a welcome release.

The full sermon title of the Hadley sermon was, "Of Those Who Walk in the Light of God's Countenance."[48] The text is, "Blessed *is* the people that know the joyful sound: they shall walk, O Lord, in the light of thy countenance" (Ps 89:15, KJV). Edwards relates the year of Jubilee and the sounding of trumpets as a joyous occasion. He then moves quickly to claim that this type represents the anti-type, the "preaching of the glorious gospel," representing the "blowing of a trumpet."[49] He then turns to his Text and says, "That the gospel should be called a joyful sound, and it is spoken of as 'glad tidings of great joy'" (Luke 2:10, KJV).[50] Further, Edwards seems to allude to his May, 1731, sermon, "Christians a Chosen Generation" (1 Pet 2:9).[51] He ties these terms of oneness together as, "The joyful sound of the gospel is the means of gathering them [together]; (Heb. 12:22, 'ye are come [unto mount Sion']."[52]

Edwards may have made subtle reference to his views of church communion in the Application section under I. of Self-Examination.

---

47. Minkema, *Chronology*, 21-27.

48. Jonathan Edwards, "Of Those Who Walk in the Light of God's Countenance," in *Works of Jonathan Edwards, Sermons and Discourses, 1743-1758*, ed. Wilson H. Kimnach (New Haven, CT: Yale University Press, 2006), 25:701.

49. Ibid.

50. Ibid., 702.

51. Jonathan Edwards, "Christians: A Chosen Generation," in *Works of Jonathan Edwards: Sermons and Discourses, 1730-1733*, ed. Mark Valeri (New Haven, CT: Yale University Press, 1999), 17:276, 307. He cites 1 Pet 2:9 in this sermon, and mentions "one nation, one society or people, etc."

52. Edwards, "God's Countenance," 25:707.

Whether you know the joyful sound. Do you understand? Have you truly received and embraced it? Do you habitually embrace it? Is it truly such a joyful sound to you? [Is it as] joyful to you as to the shepherds, [or] to the heavenly hosts? Are you truly united to that people? [Are you] related to 'em by birth; [do you] cleave to the head of that society [and] submit to the laws, your heart united to them? I Cor. 12:25-26…What a joyful sound will you hear in the conclusion of all things, when the final sentence is passed.[53]

The "birth" that Edwards is referring to in the application section is spiritual in nature. The communion controversy revolved around true profession of faith and Congregational doctrines that made claims to physical birth and association to the Church through the sacraments.

As the spiritual leader of the home, the head of the family offered the child for baptism. However, Edwards inquires, "do you cleave to the head of that society?"[54] Naturally, he is referring to Christ and the new birth for salvation. The probable implication he is making is entrance into the "society" (church) via the new birth, not an entitlement through physical birth and infant baptism. Precisely, as Edwards had given a defense of his Calvinistic views on July 8, 1731, in Boston, without ever mentioning the terms "Arminianism" and "Calvinism," he is meticulous in alluding to his views on a regenerate church membership, without ever mentioning the name of "Stoddard" or his own term "Qualifications for Full Communion." Edwards's homiletics were still taking aim and hitting the mark, but Winslow appears to fall short of the mark when she claimed, "with the removal to Stockbridge his preaching days were definitely over."[55]

---

53. Ibid., 708-09.
54. Ibid., 708.
55. Winslow, *Jonathan Edwards*, 262.

## EDWARDS'S RE-PREACHING OF EARLIER SERMONS

Jonathan Edwards's activities in Stockbridge included keeping up with two congregations, dealing with external community problems, writing his major works, and—at a moment's notice—having to think of strategies for the possibility of imminent attacks. With all of these dynamics in his life, it is understandable that he would lean frequently upon his vast sermon corpus for the sermons preached to the English congregation. As he continued to master the sermon form by the late 1730s and through the 1740s, his new developmental process involved effectively communicating to the Indians. By 1756, it is apparent that he was juggling his multifaceted ministry with efficiency and awareness.

Re-preaching earlier sermons was simply his way of putting each piece of his spiritual and administrative puzzle into their proper slots. On a positive note, Winslow commends Edwards:

> His analysis of the mission problem, past, present, future, political and educational as well as religious, suggests that the trustees of New Jersey College were probably not making any mistake when, too late, they invited him to take charge as president. He had the detachment of the administrator, and saw the problem which lay underneath the details of a given situation . . . but he could also balance a budget, plan a vocational course of study for those whose I.Q.'s were on the minus side, and direct mission activities with reference to the daily lives of those for whom it existed, as well as preach toward their eventual Christianization.[56]

Therefore, Edwards did not re-preach earlier sermons at Stockbridge because of administrative inadequacies, personal apathy, lack of concern for the English congregation, a sense of self-righteousness that he had arrived, or in order that he might have more time to write "Freedom of

---

56. Ibid., 257-58.

the Will" and "Original Sin." He re-preached them, possibly because he could simultaneously provide a diet of substance to the English congregation and still develop as a missionary preacher, while taking care of other administrative responsibilities to the Indians and writing other major works.

Instead of neglecting one for the other, he chose to give both what they needed—the Word of God preached on each congregation's level. Furthermore, because of the availability of his notebooks and so much sermon material from Edwards's lengthy preaching career, one can understand his ability to adapt to differing audiences and congregations when it came to substance and clarity. Wheeler claims, "The Stockbridge sermons rest on the power of images and stories, freed of the first person narrative scaffolding of his earlier sermons . . . the sermons tell us not only of the workings of Edwards' mind but the shift in rhetorical style necessitated by a change in audience."[57]

## JONAH 3:10: RE-PREACHED IN 1756

Originally, Edwards preached this sermon on December 21, 1727, following an earthquake that shook Northampton on October 29, 1727. The title is "When God Gives Sinful People Warnings of Impending Judgments the Only Way to Have Them Averted Is Reformation."[58] The Text was: "And God saw their works, that they turned from their evil way; and God repented of the evil, that he had said that he would do unto them; and he did it not" (Jonah 3:10, KJV).

The original manuscript is a duodecimo, but is sized smaller than others

---

57. Wheeler, "Living upon Hope," 137.

58. Jonathan Edwards, "When God Gives Sinful People Warnings of Impending Judgments, The Only Way to Have Them Averted Is Reformation, Jonah 3:10)," *Writings of Jonathan Edwards*, Gen MSS 151, Box 13, Folder 1013 (New Haven, CT: Yale University, Beinecke Library Rare Books and Manuscripts, 1720's Sermons).

at 4.25 X 4'. The Doctrine section is on the third page, and the Roman numeral I. says Prop., written in rather large letters. The Application section begins at the bottom of page sixteen, written in large letters also. Edwards's reference to Zechariah 5:2-4 is written clearly, followed by two horizontal lines.

The sermon is very clean, and does not have as many horizontal lines as later sermons. Several entire pages are free from any horizontal lines, and he threaded the sermon leaves in the middle of the pages only. This is different from many of his later sermons that he threaded from top to bottom with a knot in the center.[59] The sermon is laid out in Edwards's usual Text, Doctrine, and Application divisions. He points out two basic things about the text as being "God's expression of 'mercy towards them', and Nineveh's repentance regarding their sin."[60]

In the doctrine section, Edwards points out that, often before judging a people, God gives them warning. Often, God gives warnings in the form of general, impending, and great judgments. Sometimes, God gives them to a neighboring people, and he gives warning of impending judgments through his messengers. Additionally, God may give warnings through "strange sights in the heavens, and sometimes by earthquakes, as it was before the destruction of Jerusalem, and were sent for signs of it" (Luke 21:11).[61] Further, Edwards deals with the true intentions of the human heart toward God:

> A people's praying that judgments may be averted is insufficient. For a people to pray to God that he would not punish them for their sins, and all the while to go on sinning and provoking God as much as ever, is a piece of mockery, and we can't expect but that God by such prayers will be more provoked and his anger

---

59. Edwards, "Impending Judgments," Jonathan Edwards Collection.
60. Jonathan Edwards, "Impending Judgments Averted Only by Reformation," in *Works of Jonathan Edwards: Sermons and Discourses, 1723-1729*, ed. Kenneth P. Minkema (New Haven, CT: Yale University Press, 1997), 14:217.
61. Ibid., 218-20.

enflamed instead of being turned away.[62]

In other words, "fasting," "sacrifices," "vain oblations," and other things, in the absence of true repentance, will cause God to "hide" his "eyes from you."[63]

In the Application, Edwards argues "both the mercy and justice of God."[64] He reminds his audience that God has had mercy on them, but that now he had warned them "by shaking the earth under us, by shaking the whole land and some parts of it more frequently and in a more awful manner."[65] Additionally, he cites specific sins that were common in New England, such as "swearing, cursing, especially among the young people. Intemperance, drunkenness.... Abundantly more frequent are the out breakings of lasciviousness and whoredom of late years than before."[66] He urges them to "forsake your evil ways," because "he remembers the sin you commit in secret."[67]

Edwards was always opportunistic in his preaching with regard to natural disasters, wars, and calamities. Preachers in the seventeenth century and the early eighteenth century looked at these things as warnings from Almighty God. Often, the modern press ridicules preachers in the twenty-first century who take this approach as being unloving and insensitive.[68] This particular sermon on "Impending Judgments" gives insights into Edwards's theological views regarding the sovereignty of God

---

62. Ibid., 221.
63. Ibid.
64. Ibid., 223.
65. Ibid., 224.
66. Ibid., 225.
67. Ibid., 226.
68. Following the events of 9-11-2001, the now deceased Jerry Falwell Sr., received heavy criticism for remarks he made on Fox News regarding God's judgment on America in that event. Postmodern America has become very intolerant of considering national tragedies as the judgment of God. However, in studying the Old Testament prophets, Edwards understood that one could not avoid the reality of the judgment of God upon the nations for their sins.

and his righteous justice and judgment in the midst of calamity.

When Jonathan Edwards first preached this sermon on Jonah 3:10, on December 21, 1727, the recent event was the earthquake that had occurred on October 29, 1727. Edwards probably chose this sermon to re-preach in January, of 1756, because of the "threatening of the calamities of war."[69] However, another earthquake had occurred in New England on November 18, 1755, that may have reminded Edwards of his Jonah 3:10 message.[70] He then reached back almost thirty years in his sermon file, in order to preach this sermon on "Impending Judgments."

In Edwards's letters, it is apparent that the threat of Stockbridge's invasion, in 1756, was prominent in his mind for several years. On April 10, 1756, to the Rev. William McCulloch, Edwards writes:

> With respect to the situation of Stockbridge; it is not in the province of New York as you have been informed, but in the utmost border of the province of the Massachusetts on the west, next to the province of New York; about forty miles west of Connecticut River, about twenty-five miles east of Hudson's River, and about thirty-five miles southeast from Albany. A place exposed in this time of war. Four persons were killed here in the beginning of September 1754, by Canada Indians; which occasioned a great alarm to us and great part of New England. Since this we have had many alarms; but God has preserved us. I desire your prayers that we may still be preserved, and that God would be with me and my family and people, and bless us in all respects.[71]

---

69. Edwards, "Impending Judgments," 14:218. Under the second point in Edwards's Doctrine (Jonah 3:10 message), he mentions this calamity.

70. Minkema, *Chronology*, 25.

71. Jonathan Edwards, Personal letter to Rev. William McCulloch, 11 February 1757, in *Works of Jonathan Edwards: Letters and Personal Writings, Personal Narrative*, ed. George S. Claghorn (New Haven, CT: Yale University Press, 1998), 16:687.

Along with all of his concerns for two congregations—the troubles with Indian relations, the financial strains, writing his major works, and keeping up with correspondence, Edwards was in constant prayer for the safety of his immediate family, due to the threat of invasion.

In many ways, the world Edwards lived in at Stockbridge was uncertain and unstable. Letters and information traveled at the pace of a horse, and knowing the movement of armies and Indian invaders was difficult, to say the least. Even if the messenger warning of approaching danger arrived, he might be too late. Perhaps those who criticize Edwards for re-preaching a few old sermons should take more time to consider the dangerous historical context in which he lived, and focus more on the efforts of Jonathan Edwards, the missionary pastor, administrator, and voluminous writer.

## Farewell Sermons to Stockbridge— January 15, 1758

On September 29, 1757, the trustees at the College of New Jersey, in Princeton, wrote and delivered their decision to ask Jonathan Edwards to "succeed his son-in law," Aaron Burr, who died on September 24, 1757, at the age of forty-one.[72] Almost seven years after accepting his call to Stockbridge, a council of ministers convened, at Edwards's request, to discuss and decide on his future with the college. Edwards left the decision in their hands, and when they announced their judgment, Edwards wept.[73] On January 15, 1758, he delivered his farewell sermons to the English and Indian congregations at Stockbridge.

The sermon title for the English congregation was from the text, "Watch ye therefore, and pray always, that ye may be accounted worthy to escape all these things that shall come to pass, and to stand before the

---

72. Marsden, *Jonathan Edwards*, 429.
73. Ibid., 431.

Son of man" (Luke 21:36, KJV).[74] Edwards began by telling them that "many dreadful things are coming upon this wicked world. The righteous, and they only, shall be thought fit to escape those things that shall come. And all at last must be called to appear before Christ."[75] He concluded by telling them to "watch, pray, always," and in the Application he closed by discussing "what must watch against," and "What need of watching. Always. Prayer."[76]

The wording of the English farewell sermon is rough, because the sermon is simply a skeletal outline. Once again, these two sermons exemplify the external reduction of Edwards's sermons. However, at this point in Edwards's preaching career, he had mastered being able to preach extensive sermons through his erudition, without having to carry the multiple-page duodecimo sermons into the pulpit. He came prepared in a different way than from his days at Northampton as Stoddard's protégé and understudy. His mind was now a storehouse of information from his years of experience and study. He had developed his own form of extemporaneous delivery, formed from his own preaching lab. He was content and confident with various types of audiences, and had preached before the elite of New Haven and Boston, the Congregationalists of Northampton, the rural at Enfield, the Presbyterians of New York and New Jersey, and the Indian mission at Stockbridge. In these final exhortations, he left both of the congregations with words of warning, as well as encouragement.

The sermon title for the Indians was, "God's People Should Remember Them that Have Been Their Ministers." The Scripture text for this sermon was: "Remember them that have the rule over you, who have spoken to you the word of God; whose faith follow, considering the end of their conversation. Jesus Christ the same yesterday, and today, for forever" (Heb

---

74. Jonathan Edwards, "Watch and Pray Always (Luke 21:36)," in *Works of Jonathan Edwards, Sermons and Discourses, 1743-1758*, ed. Wilson H. Kimnach (New Haven, CT: Yale University Press, 2006), 25:716.

75. Ibid.

76. Ibid. Edwards shortened his language in these sermon lines.

13:7-8, KJV). The sermon is now separated in two geographical locations, "a single quarto leaf in the collection of the Andover Newton Theological School and a two-leaf fold in Yale's Beinecke Library."[77]

The two-leaf fold at the Beinecke Library in New Haven, Connecticut, has the appearance of a skeletal outline, basically with one major thought per page. The sermon is an odd size of 6' X 4'. Upon first glance, it is evident that other segments of the sermon are missing.[78] The first page begins with the Roman numeral II, and the second page begins with the Roman numeral III. Roman numeral II says, "A minister if they are faithful workers, [will] come to an happy end of life [and] work, they also that follow this [Edwards appears to mention a name at the end, but it is too difficult to discern]."[79]

The Andover Newton portion that Kimnach presents has several of Edwards's same thoughts from his Northampton "Farewell." His first point under the text says, "They have been God's messengers." The second point says, "because the ministers that have spoken to them the word of God have labored for their greatest good." The third point says, "God will remember, and call 'em to an account," probably referring to the foes of the mission in Stockbridge.[80] Additionally, he urges the Indians not to listen to these enemies of the mission if "any talk

---

77. Wilson H. Kimnach, Introduction to "God's People Should Remember Them that Have Been Their Ministers," in *Works of Jonathan Edwards, Sermons and Discourses, 1743-1758*, ed. Wilson H. Kimnach (New Haven, CT: Yale University Press, 2006), 25:712.

78. The other segments are in the Andover Newton Theological School collection. See ibid., fn 65.

79. Jonathan Edwards, "God's People Should Remember Them that Have Been Their Ministers (Heb 13:7-8)," Jonathan Edwards Collection, MSS 151, Box 14, Folder 1128 (New Haven, CT: Yale University, Beinecke Library, May 1742). The writer examined this sermon at the Beinecke Library, Yale University, September, of 2009. Edwards's handwriting was not clear enough to discern the name.

80. Jonathan Edwards, "Farewell to the Indians," in *Works of Jonathan Edwards: Sermons and Discourses, 1743-1758*, ed. Wilson H. Kimnach (New Haven, CT: Yale University Press, 2006), 25:713.

against" the "next minister," claiming that "he is good for nothing, don't mind them."[81]

The Andover Newton portion ends with overtones of the Northampton "Farewell Sermon." "Whether we shall ever see each other in this world is uncertain: but remember we must meet again at the last day."[82] Edwards always seemed to preach each sermon as if it were his last, probably because of the unstable world in which he lived. However, this time his uncertainty about life in "this world" was drawing closer to becoming a reality. His days of adapting, developing, and delivering sermons would soon be coming to an unexpected end. Nevertheless, Edwards was always opportunistic about God's new appointments. In his farewell sermon to the Indians, some "pros" and "cons" are written regarding his move to Princeton. "Not have so much to say…7. There can have Books…8. Trustees willing to favour me as to my studies.…Advantages to do good…10. Prevent Evil […] divert me? From study & writing."[83]

For one last time, and one last appointment, Edwards would ponder through his analytical skills the possibilities of his new position at Princeton. History was moving forward, and he was hoping and praying for a lifespan similar to his father who was recently deceased. If God's providence allowed, he knew he would accomplish his desired task before moving up to his eternal reward. From his perspective, this would involve "study and writing."[84]

Although as he rode off from Stockbridge, with his sights fixed on his future at Princeton, Edwards must have felt a sense of satisfaction gained from his life as pastor and missionary. Of his efforts, Wheeler

---

81. Ibid., 714.
82. Ibid.
83. Ibid. Kimnach says, "JE had used the sheet out of which part of this sermon was made to construct a list of advantages and disadvantages of the Princeton position. The end of the 'pros' continues to the bottom of this page, and the 'cons' begin on the next."
84. Ibid.

acknowledged that he "stood as an apostle of Christ and bid the Indians join the nation of the elect."[85] Although many of the English looked down on the Indians, Edwards viewed things through a theological mindset. Wheeler gave a reminder of how closely Edwards actually saw the relationship of all people through the doctrine of original sin and "depravity."[86]

He denied the Arminians' faith in the ability of the individual to effect salvation and also the deist claims for natural human reason to discover ultimate, divine truths in the contemplation of the physical world. In reaching and demonstrating this proposition, Edwards' encounter with the Indians was a crucial component. Edwards wanted to remind his readers that all good gifts are from above—that the English are not innately superior to the Indians. The barbarity of the Indians should be cause for thanking God for his gift of revelation, and a reminder that it is only the grace of God that separates English and Indian.[87]

By the time Edwards left for Princeton, he had preached to the "congregation of Stockbridge and Mohawk Indians at least 226 times."[88] The experience in Stockbridge had been another challenge, but he was not leaving without a harvest. He knew his labors had not been in vain, because he had witnessed transformation of lives following his preaching. As always, for Edwards, God was the one to receive glory in man's redemption, whether that man was English or Indian. His wife and children, whom he left behind in Stockbridge, waved goodbye for the final time, as Edwards turned and gave his final exhortation to them. Susannah later wrote, "As affectionately, as if he should not come again, when he was outside the house, he turned and declared, 'I commit you to God'."[89]

---

85. Wheeler, "Living upon Hope," 191.
86. Ibid., 194.
87. Ibid., 194-95.
88. Ibid., 162.
89. Marsden, *Jonathan Edwards*, 491.

# Stockbridge: Contemporary Application of Maturation That Results in Transitional Abilities

Stockbridge and Princeton were two different types of service. The focus of Stockbridge was upon two local churches, and at Princeton, the focus was the College of New Jersey. Obviously, no one will ever be able to live the same life that Jonathan Edwards lived. Nevertheless, many of the events that transpired in his life have modern correlations and educational application. For instance, Edwards was thrust into a new culture and situation in Stockbridge following his Northampton termination. His ministry to the Indian and English congregations was probably not what he would have predicted five years earlier. On the other hand, his final destination to Princeton by this point in his life seemed suitable for a pastor and intellectual theologian like Edwards.

The new ministry situation in Stockbridge eventually revealed much about the heart and character of Jonathan Edwards. Later, the position he held for a brief time at Princeton reflects even more about his maturation level and his transitional abilities. An appropriate description of these final two places of service for Edwards is transitional abilities and adaptability. He once again was able to draw from his past experiences and knowledge and apply them in a present situation.

## Applying Transitional Abilities in the Contemporary

When a minister settled into his first church in eighteenth-century Massachusetts, a good chance existed that he would pastor at that church until his death. Jonathan Edwards's father, Timothy, and his grandfather, Solomon Stoddard, would both end their lives as classic examples of that trend. In Jonathan Edwards's mind in the late 1720s, when he was settled as pastor in Northampton, he possibly envisioned serving and eventually dying in Northampton where his Grandfather Stoddard eventually died and was buried.

However, in the twenty-first century, dynamics are much different regarding tenures in churches. Presently, a minister staying in a church for more than five years is considered beyond the norm.[90] Consequently, it is common for individuals to be placed in numerous towns, cities, and states during the course of their ministry. Therefore, learning from Edwards's efficiency in sermon preparation and delivery and ministry, may help one's effectiveness to transition from one ministry to another. Due to the many facets and responsibilities of ministry today, having an ability to develop a system of preparation and delivery will enable one to utilize precious time within a busy schedule. Adaptability has taken on a new perspective in this day and age because of the transient nature of families, jobs, and staff positions. Studying and delivering sermons weekly can be an overwhelming responsibility. Vines and Shaddix appropriately claimed, "Men prepare sermons; God prepares men. The man who would preach, then, has the responsibility of learning to prepare."[91]

Thousands of ministers drop out of the ministry every year, and one key reason is "burnout." "According to a recent article, thirty three percent of pastors felt burned out within the first five years of ministry. The same percentage also said that being in ministry is a hazard to their [sic] family."[92] Edwards may have felt these same pressures upon leaving Northampton, but he maintained the course. Similarly, those who work through difficult situations often find that they return to satisfaction later

---

90. Barna Group, "A Profile of Protestant Pastors in Anticipation of 'Pastor Appreciation Month'" [on-line]; accessed February 12, 2012; available at http://www.barna.org/barna-update/article/5-barna-update/59-a-profile-of-protestant-pastors-in-anticipation-of-qpastor-appreciation-monthq?q=years+ service; Internet.

91. Vines and Shaddix, Introduction to *Power in the Pulpit*, 13.

92. Daniel Sherman, "Pastor Burnout Statistics" [on-line]; accessed February 12, 2012; available at http://www.pastorburnout.com/pastor-burnout-statistics.html; Internet.

by persevering through a major trial. Continuing to apply these developmental stages and drawing from Edwards's life experiences have the potential of playing an encouraging role. Even after Edwards left Northampton and went to Stockbridge, his problems in ministry did not cease. He continued to put his plethora of gifts to work and shared them successfully with an English-speaking and Indian congregation, of which contemporaries should take heart.

## Keys to Transitioning to a New Audience Using Edwards's Stockbridge Model

Since Jonathan Edwards had honed many of his skills in by the time he reached Stockbridge, he was eventually able to modify his sermons to each congregation. As previously mentioned, he re-preached many of his sermons, but learned to use examples from nature and life to connect with the Indians. Kroll mentions three important relationships with today's effective communicators and their audiences.

> It does not take an audience long, however, to determine whether or not you are speaking from a sincere heart.... It is essential that a speaker have a genuine love for his audience.... Whatever system or method is used, the preacher must analyze his audience to determine his approach to presenting truth to them.... He must gather material accordingly, plan his sermon accordingly, and preach accordingly.... A speaker is not to be controlled by his audience, but, by the same token, he is not to be oblivious to their needs.... He needs to adjust to the audience.[93]

Kroll's three qualities could be considered universal for every generation of communicators. A genuine love for the audience, an analytical ability

---

93. Kroll, *Prescription for Preaching*, 111-13.

with one's audience, and then adjusting to the audience are all important to consider, along with the previously mentioned four stages. In other words, these three qualities Kroll mentions may be juxtaposed with the intellectual understanding of the other developmental stages in order to transition effectively.

Therefore, Edwards had acquired most of the intellectual tools at this point to apply to his situation. However, the dynamics of handling two congregations with different cultures and languages would take skill. Edwards had not acquired some skills at this point. First, he lacked a working knowledge of the Mohican language. Second, he understood how to apply his skills to an English-speaking people, but he may have experienced difficulty in even understanding the nonverbal and verbal feedback of his Indian congregation. This would be a new learning curve for him. Some of his strategies would include locating a good Indian interpreter for preaching, adaptation of his sermons in content and length, staying connected to the Indian community by living near them, and being involved in their daily education and well-being.

Today in the United States, many American English-speaking pastors are finding themselves in similar situations, especially with the increasing Hispanic population. These transitional methods used by Edwards are still applicable today. The writer's church has recently commenced an ESL program in order to help local Hispanics learn the English language. Through this program, the church is reaching out to them through education and Gospel presentation.

Furthermore, the Church in America today should be understanding that home missions on its own soil has expanded in recent years to a foreign mission field at home. Consequently, Edwards's life and ministry among the Indians at Stockbridge is a story that is not only interesting, but it also has an educational value today for those interested in evangelizing other cultures within American society by utilizing some of his strategies to reach them with the Gospel.

## A College President (Princeton)

In August, of 1757, Aaron Burr, who was married to Edwards's daughter Esther, visited Stockbridge.[94] The following month, on September 4, though weak and ill, Burr had to ride many miles from his New Jersey home in order to preach Governor Belcher's funeral service. After arriving back home by September 5, Burr succumbed to death by a fever on September 24, 1757.[95] Less than a week later, on September 29, the trustees sent word to Jonathan Edwards requesting that he consider filling the office of president at the College of New Jersey.

In Edwards's letter of response, he seems to discourage their consideration of him, writing the following words:

> Reverend and Honored Gentlemen, I was not a little surprised, on receiving the unexpected notice of your having made choice of me to succeed the late President [Aaron] Burr, as the head of Nassau Hall.... The chief difficulty in my mind, in the way of accepting this important and arduous office, are these two: first my own defects, unfitting me for such an undertaking, many of which are generally known; besides other, which my own heart is conscious to. I have a constitution in many respects peculiar unhappy, attended with flaccid solids, vapid sizy and scarce fluid, and a low tide of spirits; often occasioning a kind of childish weakness and contemptibleness of speech, presence, and demeanor; with a disagreeable dullness and stiffness, much unfitting me for conversation, but more especially for the government of a college.... I am also deficient in some parts

---

94. Minkema, *Chronology*, 26.
95. Esther Burr, "September 2, 1757 Entry," *Journal of Esther Burr*, ed. Jeremiah Eames Ranking, 93 [on-line]; accessed December 28, 2009; available at Books.google.com; Internet.

of learning, particularly in algebra, and the higher parts of mathematics, and in the Greek classics; my Greek learning having been chiefly in the New Testament."[96]

This certainly does not sound like a man with ambitious desires; rather, Edwards humbly lays out many of his negative physiological and academic shortcomings. Later in the letter, he even tells them, "On the whole, I am much at a loss, with respect to the way of my duty in this important affair: I am in doubt, whether if I should engage in it, I should not do what both you and I should be sorry for afterwards."[97]

Additionally, for almost seven years, Edwards and his family had settled in Stockbridge, acquiring a home and land among the inhabitants.[98] Regarding these circumstances, he tells them, "I have in the world (without any prospect of disposing of it, under present circumstances, without losing it, in great part) now when we have scarcely got over the trouble and damage sustained by our removal from Northampton."[99] Regardless of all of these perhaps exaggerated inadequacies, the trustees serving the College of New Jersey desired Edwards to come to Nassau Hall as quickly as possible.

## EDWARDS'S FIRST SERMON AT NASSAU HALL

Upon arriving at Princeton, Jonathan Edwards preached his first sermon at the College of New Jersey on "Jesus Christ the same yesterday,

---

96. Jonathan Edwards, "Letter to the Trustees of the College of New Jersey," in *Works of Jonathan Edwards, Letters and Writings*, ed. George S. Claghorn (New Haven, CT: Yale University Press, 1998), 16:726.
97. Ibid., 729.
98. Winslow, *Jonathan Edwards*, 287. Winslow says, "He owned his homestead and several hundred acres of land, enough to take care of his needs."
99. Jonathan Edwards, "Letter to the Trustees," 16:725-26.

and today, and forever" (Heb 13:8, KJV). Winslow says, "For his very brief term of active service, there is record of a sermon preached in the College Hall."[100] However, she does not cite a Scripture text. Murray does cite the Hebrews 13:8 verse, and claimed that when this sermon was concluded,

> his hearers were surprised to discover that two hours had passed so quickly. Thereafter, he preached each Sunday in the College hall, and introduced the senior class to questions in divinity for which they had to prepare answers later to be discussed in class, a procedure which met with an enthusiastic response.[101]

Edwards may have felt a sense of energy around the students. Many of the students had experienced the previous year's revival, and now they were sitting under the tutelage of one of the most well-known pastor/theologians of their time. The fact that "two hours had passed so quickly" gives one the idea that Edwards's words were filled with knowledge and interest. Because of the many years of preaching and teaching lessons to young people of differing ages at home and in the Congregational Church, speaking to a group of students came natural for Edwards. Additionally, he had spent time at Yale as a tutor, and his experiences in higher learning gave him an ability to have a thorough understanding of diverse audiences. Everything Edwards had been through in his fifty-four-year journey had prepared him for this moment. Ezra Stiles probably misread Edwards when he said, "The volatility of 100 youth would have disturbed his calm quiet and made him unhappy."[102] Hopkins's words discredit assumptions such as these when he wrote:

> During this time, Mr. Edwards seemed to enjoy an uncommon degree of the presence of God. He told his daughters he had had great exercise, concern, and fear, relative to his engaging in that business; but since it now appeared, so far as he could see, that

---

100. Winslow, *Jonathan Edwards*, 290.
101. Murray, *Jonathan Edwards*, 440.
102. Ezra Stiles, "May 24, 1779 Entry," in *The Literary Diary of Ezra Stiles*, ed. Franklin B. Dexter (New York: Scribner's, 1901), 2:337.

he was called of God to that place and work, he did cheerfully devote himself to it, leaving himself and the event with God, to order what seemed to him good.[103]

## Edwards as a Proficient Preacher

Many of Edwards's critics do not agree that he ever developed to the status of a proficient preacher, a proficient preacher defined as one who has the ability to study for a sermon, write down a skeletal outline, and preach from his intellectual overflow by either glancing at the outline or preaching memoriter. By the time he arrived in Princeton, New Jersey, adequate evidence seems to argue that Jonathan Edwards had achieved this status.

To be fair and objective, there is no denying that Edwards never reached the impressiveness of George Whitefield's charisma. On the other hand, however, it is a caricature to describe him as Drummond surmised, "We would hardly have called him a dynamic preacher. He laboriously read every word from a manuscript. Not only that, his eyesight and writing were so poor he held the manuscript only inches from his nose, rarely looking at the congregation. The message was Calvinistic and hell fire!"[104]

First, assuming that Edwards's eyesight worsened with age makes no sense regarding his sermon corpus. He wrote his early octavo sermons in larger handwriting, and his later duodecimo sermons in smaller handwriting. If Edwards's eyes had worsened with age, it would seem logical that he would have maintained the octavo size for easier reading. However, since Edwards went to the smaller duodecimo sermons as he aged, Drummonds's argument seems contrary to the chronological manuscript

---

103. Hopkins, *Life and Character*, 85.
104. Lewis A. Drummond, *The Awakening that Must Come* (Nashville: Broadman Press, 1978), 13.

evidence. Second, his statement about Edwards holding the manuscript "inches from his nose, rarely looking at the congregation" comes with no citation of a source.[105]

Additionally, John E. Smith surmised, "Edwards for the most part, read his sermons, although there are indications that he would have liked to speak extemporaneously...[and] the record shows that he was not very effective as a preacher between 1742 and his dismissal from Northampton in 1750."[106] Smith's first statement is typical of many who often make general statements about Edwards's preaching without clarification. Some truth exists to his statement, but obviously the statement does not consider the entire developmental span of Edwards's ministry. Second, from 1742 until his dismissal, Edwards was an effective preacher, although he was not well received by his congregation in 1750, due to the controversy. Smith appears to base his argument on the historical tragedy, rather than the sermonic evidence.

Perhaps Edwards's daughter, Esther, who sat under his preaching until she married Aaron Burr during the Stockbridge era, gives a more accurate and objective understanding of his preaching:

> When he is speaking in the pulpit, it often seems that his voice has a supernatural, an angelic tenderness and authority. There is in his utterance no weakness or softness, though it is not a loud voice nor very masculine. There is such a holy loyalty to the truth in the speaker, as though he were one of God's swift messengers, unwinged indeed, save in the Spirit, which often tries lofty flights, but coming straight from the ineffable glory, commissioned of infinite love to proclaim the truth and defend it.[107]

---

105. Ibid., 13, 146.

106. John E. Smith, *Jonathan Edwards: Puritan, Preacher, Philosopher* (Notre Dame, IN: University of Notre Dame Press, 1992), 139.

107. Esther Burr, "1751 Entry," *Journal of Esther Burr*, ed. Jeremiah Eames Ranking, 47 [on-line]; accessed December 28, 2009; available at Books.google.com; Internet.

In late August, of 1752, Edwards had, at this earlier date, preached in Newark, to the students at the College of New Jersey.[108] Additionally, Esther heard her father preach at Newark, New Jersey, on September 28, 1752, before the Presbyterian Synod of New York. She wrote her thoughts following his sermon as a reinvigorating experience: "It has been a great refreshment to my soul, today, to hear again Mr. Edwards, my honored father, from the pulpit. I still think there is none like him." Edwards had preached a sermon at the Synod from the text, "Thou believest that there is one God; thou doest well; the devils also believe and tremble" (James 2:19, KJV). The title of his message was "True Grace, Distinguished from the Experience of Devils."[109] Kimnach claims that,

> Edwards' selection of the sermon on Jas. 2:19 for repreaching before a learned and influential audience at the 1752 synod is open to question.... If nothing else, Edwards may have wanted to sum up his preaching before an audience that might pay for the publication of it. And in fact, True Grace proved to be the last sermon he published.[110]

Three years later, on September 20, 1755, Edwards was back in Newark with the Burr's to attend commencement and travel to Philadelphia for the Presbyterian Synod, beginning on October 1, 1755.[111] Marsden speculates:

> If ever Edwards met Benjamin Franklin, it would have been on this visit to Philadelphia. Franklin had published and even read some of Edwards' works, and the circles of elite men in Philadelphia were not large. If they did meet, their conversation

---

108. Minkema, *Chronology*, 22.

109. Jonathan Edwards, "True Grace, Distinguished from the Experience of Devils," in *Works of Jonathan Edwards: Sermons and Discourses, 1743-1758*, ed. Wilson H. Kimnach (New Haven, CT: Yale University Press, 2006), 25:608.

110. Wilson H. Kimnach, Introduction to "True Grace, Distinguished from the Experience of Devils," in *Works of Jonathan Edwards: Sermons and Discourses, 1743-1758*, ed. Wilson H. Kimnach (New Haven, CT: Yale University Press, 2006), 25:606-07.

111. Minkema, *Chronology*, 25.

may have included talk of their mutual friendship with Whitefield and shared intelligence about the military situation since the battle of Lake George.[112]

Additionally, whether or not it had entered Edwards's mind, the Presbyterian brethren may already have been contemplating some way to involve Jonathan Edwards with the college. The fact that they moved so quickly following Burr's death seems to support the idea.

Giving consideration to the above historical information about Edwards's numerous contacts with the Presbyterian Synod and the College of New Jersey, more than likely, perhaps one can conclude that several of the students Edwards addressed when taking over the presidency had heard him preach previously. Inwardly Edwards was cautious, but his first performance at Princeton seems to reveal that he was ready to preach, teach, guide, and administer the students and find time to complete the writing of his major works. Furthermore, his vast experience with sermons, treatises, spiritual awakenings, academic addresses at Yale and Harvard, missionary work among the Indians, and relationships and correspondence to influential people in the Colonies, gave him one of the best resumes in New England.

However, out of all of these categories, Edwards had the most experience with preparing sermons and preaching. He had developed the skills of a proficient-preacher, and the reaction of these students at the college—and those like Esther Edwards Burr and Samuel Hopkins—who had heard him numerous times, seem to testify to this fact. By 1758, one can perhaps argue that Edwards had developed his ability to prepare a full sermon manuscript, semi-manuscript, skeletal outline, and preach extempore. Additionally, his listeners and colleagues gave affirmation that he had an advanced ability. After preaching on the same day as Jonathan Edwards, Samuel Hopkins said the comparison between his sermon and Edwards "made him ashamed."[113]

---

112. Marsden, *Jonathan Edwards*, 419.
113. Burr, "1751 Entry," 25, Internet.

According to some, Edwards had a pleasant voice and enunciation that was more than adequate for preaching his sermons. Due to his erratic health and lack of a deep voice, obviously, he often had difficulty in comparison to Whitefield's voice projection. According to evidence, the Whitefield model outperformed that of Edwards in gesture, rhythm, and charisma. However, ever since 1758, when Jonathan Edwards preached his last sermon on American soil, neither Wesley, Finney, Sunday, or Graham have rivaled Edwards's use of language. Joseph Tracy called him "perhaps the most efficient preacher in New England,"[114] and from his days as the protégé of his father and grandfather, Edwards was gifted by Divine Providence with the art of language.

However, Edwards had to work at developing his sermon form and extemporaneous delivery through stages at Northampton and Stockbridge, until he arrived at Princeton, preaching from a president's outline, while holding his audience in awe for two hours. Not only did the words simply flow from his lips at this stage in his life, his thoughts also flowed from his pen. As president, he was eager to teach and preach to his students and complete his *Summa* on the "History of Redemption."

Unfortunately, for the College of New Jersey and scholars in the coming centuries, none would be able to read Edwards's completed *Summa*. On March 22, 1758, moments before he died, he told those standing nearby, "Trust In God, and you need not fear." From his first manuscript, to his last president's outline, Jonathan Edwards stayed faithful to his calling to "preach the Word." However, death would not silence his voice. Over two hundred and fifty years later, homiletically, theologically, historically, and practically, his sermons continue to yield their impact in the twenty-first century and give evidence that his abilities moved beyond the manuscripts.

---

114. Joseph Tracy, *The Great Awakening: A History of the Revival of Religion in the Time of Edwards and Whitefield* (Boston: Tappan and Dennet, 1842), 214.

## Princeton: The Keys to Transitioning to a New Audience

On February 16, 1758, Jonathan Edwards assumed the office of President at the College of New Jersey. On March 22, 1758, he died of complications from a smallpox vaccination.[115] Edwards's time at Princeton was obviously short; however, a few items give insight into his plans and his mature abilities by this time. Furthermore, because Princeton was an educational institution, Edwards's focus would now be toward the more academic. Leading up to his transition to Princeton, he had written two recent major works. In December, of 1754, he had completed *Freedom of the Will*. In the fall following his death, *Original Sin* was published. Additionally, Edwards had plans after settling into Princeton to compile a major work of Divinity.

Furthermore, Edwards's notebooks that were produced in addition to the sermons reveal a tireless worker, but also a man of deep concern for biblical truth. Stephen J. Stein quotes one of Edwards's "Resolutions" when he said, "Resolved to study the Scriptures so steadily, constantly and frequently, as that I may find, and plainly perceive myself to grow in the knowledge of the same."[116] Stein goes on to say,

> What is remarkable is the manner in which that resolution became an actual predictor of Edwards' lifetime of activity and study. . . . Years later, looking back on that period, he recalled, "I had then, and at other times, the greatest delight in the holy Scriptures, of any book whatsoever. Oftentimes in reading it, every word seemed to touch my heart." He recalled that "every

---

115. Minkema, *Chronology*, 1.
116. Stephen J. Stein, Editor's Introduction, "The Blank Bible," in *Works of Jonathan Edwards*, vol. 24, Part I (New Haven, CT: Jonathan Edwards Center at Yale University, 2006), 5, quoting Jonathan Edwards, "Resolutions," in *Works of Jonathan Edwards, Letters and Personal Writings, Resolutions*, ed. George S. Claghorn (New Haven, CT: Yale University Press, 1998), 16:755.

sentence" seemed to communicate "a refreshing ravishing food" such that he "could not get along in reading."[117]

Regarding Edwards's reliance on Scripture, Robert Caldwell III said, "While we may not agree with all the conclusions of Edwards's theological exegesis, we should appreciate the degree to which he attempted to anchor his theology in the bedrock of Scripture."[118] This love for the Holy Scriptures over many decades produced a depth—not only in Edwards's homiletical and transitional abilities in Northampton and Stockbridge, but he also seemed to have the confidence to transfer these abilities to an educational environment at Princeton. In this final part of stage five, Edwards's biblical erudition, and his ability to transition and adapt while teaching and preaching, communicate his well-rounded mature status—even in an educational environment surrounded by college students.

## Applying Keys to Transitioning to a New Audience

Should these transitional abilities today include being able to transition from preaching in a church and then teaching in an educational institution as Jonathan Edwards attempted? Perhaps not for everyone, but Edwards's five stages of development are an example of the increasing ability to transition, adapt, and teach from one's overflow of learning. Over the years, his sermon structure served as a guide to his communication. Nevertheless, simply having a sound structure

---

117. Stein, Editor's Introduction, "Blank Bible," 24:5, quoting Jonathan Edwards, "Personal Narrative," in *Works of Jonathan Edwards: Letters and Personal Writings, Personal Narrative*, ed. George S. Claghorn (New Haven, CT: Yale University Press, 1998), 16:797.

118. Robert W. Caldwell III, Communion in the Spirit: The Holy Spirit as the Bond of Union in the Theology of Jonathan Edwards (Waynesboro, GA: Paternoster, 2006), 194.

in his manuscripts or outlines was not an end within itself. Edwards understood that sound preparation mandated a Spirit-filled presentation and a willingness to adapt to the circumstances and the audience. This was a concept he learned at an early age with his father and grandfather through his auditory experiences. Did Edwards eventually look at himself as "pastor" and "preacher" only, or did he also see himself as a "teacher?" Lucian E. Coleman Jr. made interesting observations regarding the contemporary role of the "pastor" as "teacher."

> What is even more striking is the diminished emphasis on the educational role of the pastor. The Bible provides convincing evidence that the pastors of New Testament churches were teachers. Teaching might well have been the pastor's primary ministry in many instances. The apostles were teachers. The evangelists were teachers. The Old Testament prophets so often held up as a model for contemporary ministers, functioned basically as teachers. Yet, while it is commonplace for church people to call their pastors "preacher," seldom is a minister of the gospel called "teacher."[119]

When Edwards arrived at Princeton, his past experience had given him many opportunities for preaching and teaching, but he also expressed his urge to write toward the goal of completing his major works. Therefore, his responsibility as a teacher was involved in his job description, but Edwards was also counting on having much more time to devote to writing. Murray said,

> Edwards was insistent that he could never undertake the same role as Burr. At most, if he should see light to accept their invitation, he could only undertake a general supervision of the College and certainly not teach all classes and subjects. He would perform "the whole work of a professor of divinity" but

---

119. Lucien E. Coleman Jr., *Why the Church Must Teach* (Nashville: Broadman Press, 1984), 12-13.

give no language instruction except in Hebrew.[120]

In other words, he understood which subjects were his strengths and his weaknesses and which subjects he felt comfortable teaching at the College of New Jersey. Now Edwards was ready to synthesize all of the vast knowledge he had acquired through sermon preparation and biblical study into his own Protestant version of a *Summa*, while at the same time teaching his young students his model and methods of preaching. However, according to the Providence of God to which Edwards had so trusted his entire life, he was now at the end of his own earthly pilgrimage but not without leaving his developmental stages and transitional abilities documented through his voluminous sermons, notebooks, and family history. Understanding the diversity of Edwards's life and work beyond the accusations of a "lifeless" "manuscript preacher" is to see his transitional abilities under a diversity of circumstances. The contemporary application of his transitional examples basically translate into understanding one's own past works, abilities, and experiences and maximizing those capacities to adapt to the situation at hand. Jonathan Edwards's life, works, and preaching all reveal how he desired to improve as he moved forward and to maximize his God-given abilities in every place of service, while excelling in communicating God's Word far beyond the manuscripts for the glory of God.

---

120. Murray, *Jonathan Edwards*, 437.

# CONCLUSION

Though, as has been observed, he was wont to read so considerable a part of what he delivered, yet he was far from thinking this the best way of preaching in general; and looked upon his using his notes, so much as he did, a deficiency and infirmity; and, in the latter part of his life, was inclined to think it had been better if he had never accustomed himself to use his notes at all. It appeared to him that preaching wholly without notes, agreeable to the custom in most Protestant countries, and what seems evidently to have been the manner of the apostles and primitive ministers of the gospel, was by far the most natural way, and had the greatest tendency, on the whole, to answer the end of preaching; and supposed that none who had talents equal to the work of the ministry, was incapable of speaking memoriter, if he took suitable pains for this attainment from his youth. He would have the young preacher write all his sermons, or at least most of them, out at large; and instead of reading them to his hearers, take pains to commit them to memory. Which, though it would require a great deal of labour at first, yet would soon become easier by use, and help him to speak more correctly and freely, and be of great service to him all his days.[1]

In summary, this book has made the argument that all of Jonathan Edwards's five stages of development are important and offer a model for contemporary preaching. First, auditory learning was available to those in

---

1. Hopkins, *Life and Character*, 52-53.

the eighteenth-century. Important people, church events, home visitations, and education all played a role in Edwards's auditory learning. However, in the twenty-first century, observation was made that many more audible forms are now available through modern technology. With the multiplicity of communication modes today, contemporary practitioners need not only to take advantage of these educational auditory means, but a deliberate strategy is needed to budget time into one's schedule to learn from each one. In other words, preparation for a sermon is no longer restricted to a study and sitting in front of a paperback book. While on the run, auditory technology has given outstanding means to learn on the go.

Second, moving from the auditory stage, the suggestion was made that Edwards most likely viewed Timothy Edwards's sermon manuscripts as well. The result of his auditory learning and observations in the church, his educational experiences, and his rearing in the home led to his first sermon manuscripts. As suggested, the manuscript stage of the sermon is a crucial step in one's development. However, it was suggested that to rely primarily on a manuscript over time is not ideal. Several dynamics regarding the manuscript were explained, and several arguments were presented regarding the best utility of writing a manuscript for presentation before or after the sermon itself. The evidence seems to indicate that Edwards consistently wrote his full manuscripts early in his ministry, and he probably read them as they were written. However, due to the outline forms that later appeared, the suggestion was made that he began to expand his horizons and preach with less dependence upon the manuscript. The above quote by Hopkins substantiates Edwards's desire for proficiency and his inclinations in the "latter part of his life."

Third, moving through the late 1720s and through the 1730s, Edwards's development continually moved from the manuscript to outline forms. The study suggested that he liked to experiment with the sermon form, but that Edwards was cautious not to move fully to another phase without mastering the one in the present. For important events, he still felt more comfortable writing a manuscript, but with the existence of other outline forms beginning to emerge more frequently, he may have been writing the manuscripts, but learning not to rely upon them as much during the preaching event. The primary sources presented documentation regarding Edwards using the form of a semi-manuscript as an intermediate form before actually progressing to a skeletal outline. The relevance of this stage in a contemporary way remains useful, but knowing when to transition fully from one stage to the other is important.

Fourth, beginning with the 1740s, other voices outside his family made a great impression upon him. Our study revealed how George Whitefield's preaching may have potentially stunned Edwards by an exhibition of preaching, the likes of which he had never witnessed. Whitefield was a proponent of extemporaneous preaching. Edwards was probably not just enamored; additionally, he may have desired to experiment with Whitefield's approach. This writer's conclusion regarding Edwards's experiment was that he was potentially drawn to new rhetorical tools and delivery modes, but he was aware that his communication capacities were not on the same level as Whitefield's. Nevertheless, Edwards took advantage of the learning experience from being the intellectual that he was, and he strived to be his best. This is also the timeframe during which one of his first true skeletal outlines appears from his "Sinners" sermon. This naturally leads historians and writers to speculate the purpose and the use Edwards made of the abbreviated notes. Today, Edwards's experimentation is a relevant discussion, because twenty-first-century scholars and practitioners continue to wrestle with sermon development and the most effective ways to communicate.

Finally, there are actually two parts to Edwards's final fifth stage. The first geographical location of his transitional phase occurred in Stockbridge. The second and final phase of the fifth stage occurred very briefly at Princeton, New Jersey. Within this final stage, several ideas were presented regarding Edwards's fifth developmental stage. Some say Edwards had mastered the sermon form before going to Stockbridge, while others claim that his preaching career basically came to a dead end at Stockbridge.

However, in the latter stages, this book proposed that this was another important transitional stage requiring adaptability skills on his behalf. He had the challenge of ministering and preaching to two congregations who spoke two different languages. He had the additional challenge of cultural and communication barriers. Nevertheless, Edwards not only was effective in transitioning to his new position, he adapted to the circumstances as events unfolded before him that he had never faced before.

Consequently, Edwards became a sound example for those who preach in a home or international missions setting, necessitating an adjustment to identifying effective ways to communicate the Gospel message. Further, Edwards possessed the difficult role of mediator between the Indian community and the English community in both educational and ecclesiological matters.

Further fitting within this fifth stage was his acceptance of the position as president at the College of New Jersey in Princeton. By this late moment in Edwards's life, he had settled into a role as preacher, missionary, and writer. Edwards had taken advantage of his time in Stockbridge to work on publishing new written works, as he had the opportunity to re-preach sermons. By this stage of his life, he appears to have attained excellent skills in multitasking. Despite Edwards's expression of his inadequacies to the trustees at the College of New Jersey, they must have been confident that he was up to the task and could transition to this new role, which he had never occupied previously. From his first address to the student body, all indications seem to reveal a capable intellectual, who could not only craft a sermon from its manuscript form to a skeletal outline and preach effectively from each phase in between the two, but he was also capable of transitioning from the role of "pastor" and "preacher" to that of a capable "teacher."

Unfortunately, Edwards's time as a president was brief, and he was unable to complete many of the works he desired to pen. However, he did leave voluminous works for future generations to analyze and use. Applying his five stages of development, Edwards continues to serve as a model for continual advancement in the midst of life's transitions. Implementing Edwards's stages along with the contemporary applications today, has the potential to advance individual communicators to a higher level of knowledge and maturity in an accelerated manner, progressing beyond the manuscripts as he did, while following the course of one of America's greatest preachers and theologians.

# BIBLIOGRAPHY

## Books

Adam, Peter. *Speaking God's Words*. Vancouver, BC: Regent College Publishing, 1996.

Bailey, Richard A. "Driven by Passion, Jonathan Edwards and the Art of Preaching." In *American Religion and the Evangelical Tradition, The Legacy of Jonathan Edwards*, ed. D. G. Hart, Sean Michael Lucas, and Stephen J. Nichols, 64-78. Grand Rapids: Baker Book House, 2003.

Bailey, Richard A., and Gregory A. Wills. *The Salvation of Souls*. Wheaton, IL: Crossway Books, 2002.

Beecher, Henry Ward. *Lectures on Preaching: Personal Elements in Preaching, the 1872 Yale Lectures*. London: Nelson, 1872.

Caldwell, Robert W. *Communion in the Spirit: The Holy Spirit as the Bond of Union in the Theology of Jonathan Edwards*. Waynesboro, GA: Paternoster Press, 2006.

Carrick, John. *The Preaching of Jonathan Edwards*. Edinburg: Banner of Truth Trust, 2008.

Chapell, Bryan. *Christ Centered Preaching: Redeeming the Expository Sermon*. 2nd ed. Grand Rapids: Baker Academic, 2005.

Chappell, Clovis. *Anointed to Preach*. Nashville: Abingdon Press, 1951.

Coleman, Lucien E., Jr. *Why the Church Must Teach*. Nashville: Broadman Press, 1984.

Darwin, Charles. *On the Origin of Species by Means of Natural Selection.* Charleston, SC: BiblioLife, 2009.

Davidson, Edward H. *Jonathan Edwards: The Narrative of a Puritan Mind.* Cambridge, MA: Harvard University Press, 1968.

Drummond, Lewis A. *The Awakening that Must Come.* Nashville: Broadman Press, 1978.

Edwards, Jonathan. "Aged Men and Women Joyfully Receiving Christ." In *Works of Jonathan Edwards: Sermons and Discourses, 1739-1742*, vol. 22, ed. Harry S. Stout and Nathan O. Hatch with Kyle P. Farley, 458-60. New Haven, CT: Yale University Press, 2003.

_____. "Appendix A, Preface to Discourses on Various Important Subjects." In *Works of Jonathan Edwards: Sermons and Discourses, 1734-1738*, vol. 19, ed. M. X. Lesser, 794-98. New Haven, CT: Yale University Press, 2001.

_____. Author's preface to "An Humble Inquiry into the Rules of the Word of God Concerning the Qualifications Requisite to a Compleat Standing and Full Communion in the Visible Christian Church." In *Works of Jonathan Edwards: Ecclesiastical Writings*, vol. 12, ed. David D. Hall, 167-71. New Haven, CT: Yale University Press, 1994.

_____. Author's preface to "The Period, 1730-1733." In *Works of Jonathan Edwards: Sermons and Discourses, 1730-1733*, ed. Mark Valeri, 3-34. New Haven, CT: Yale University Press, 1999.

_____. "Bringing the Ark to Zion a Second Time." In *Works of Jonathan Edwards: Sermons and Discourses, 1739-1742*, vol. 22, ed. Harry S. Stout and Nathan O. Hatch with Kyle P. Farley, 248-61. New Haven, CT: Yale University Press, 2003.

_____. *Charity and Its Fruits.* Guilford: London and Worcester, 1969.

_____. "Children Ought to Love the Lord Jesus Christ Above All." In *Works of Jonathan Edwards: Sermons and Discourses, 1739-1742*, vol. 22, ed. Harry S. Stout and Nathan O. Hatch, with Kyle P. Farley, 170-80. New Haven, CT: Yale University Press, 2003.

_____. "Christian Happiness." In *Works of Jonathan Edwards: Sermons and Discourses, 1743-1758*, vol. 25, ed. Wilson H. Kimnach, 296-310. New Haven, CT: Jonathan Edwards Center at Yale University, 1992.

_____. "Christians: A Chosen Generation." In *Works of Jonathan Edwards: Sermons and Discourses, 1730-1733*, vol. 17, ed. Mark Valeri, 276-328. New Haven, CT: Yale University Press, 1999.

_____. "The Day of Judgment." In *Works of Jonathan Edwards: Sermons and Discourses, 1723-1729*, vol. 14, ed. Kenneth P. Minkema, 506-41. New Haven, CT: Yale University Press, 1992.

_____. "Diary." In Jonathan Edwards, *Works of Jonathan Edwards: Letters and Personal Writings, Personal Narrative*, vol. 16, ed. George S. Claghorn, 759-90. New Haven, CT: Yale University Press, 1998.

_____. "A Divine and Supernatural Light." In *Works of Jonathan Edwards: Sermons and Discourses, Preface to the Period 1730-1733*, vol. 17, ed. Mark Valeri, 408-26. New Haven, CT: Yale University Press, 1999.

_____. "The Everlasting Love of God." In *Works of Jonathan Edwards: Sermons and Discourses, 1734-1738*, vol. 19, ed. M. X. Lesser, 475-90. New Haven, CT: Yale University Press, 2001.

_____. "A Farewell Sermon Preached at the First Precinct in Northampton, After the People's Public Rejection of Their Minister on June 22, 1750." In *Works of Jonathan Edwards: Sermons and Discourses, 1743-1758*, vol. 25, ed. Wilson H. Kimnach, 462-93. New Haven, CT: Jonathan Edwards Center at Yale University, 1992.

_____. "Farewell to the Indians." In *Works of Jonathan Edwards: Sermons and Discourses, 1743-1758*, vol. 25, ed. Wilson H. Kimnach, 713-14. New Haven, CT: Yale University Press, 2006.

———. "God Glorified in Man's Dependence." In *Works of Jonathan Edwards: Sermons and Discourses, 1730-1733*, vol. 17, ed. Mark Valeri, 200-216. New Haven, CT: Yale University Press, 1999.

———. "A Good Man Is a Happy Man, Whatever His Outward Condition Is." In *Works of Jonathan Edwards: Sermons and Discourses, 1720-1723*, vol. 10, ed. Wilson H. Kimnach, 296-307. New Haven, CT: Jonathan Edwards Center at Yale University, 1992.

———. "The Gospel Dispensation Is Finished Wholly and Entirely in Free and Glorious Grace." In *Works of Jonathan Edwards: Sermons and Discourses, 1743-1758*, vol. 25, ed. Wilson H. Kimnach, 390-402. New Haven, CT: Jonathan Edwards Center at Yale University, 1992.

———. "The Great Concern of a Watchman for Souls." In *Works of Jonathan Edwards: Sermons and Discourses, 1743-1758*, vol. 25, ed. Wilson H. Kimnach, 62-81. New Haven, CT: Yale University Press, 2006.

———. "Heaven's Dragnet." In *Works of Jonathan Edwards, Sermons and Discourses, 1743-1758*, vol. 25, ed. Wilson H. Kimnach, 577-81. New Haven, CT: Yale University Press, 2006.

———. "Impending Judgments Averted Only by Reformation." In *Works of Jonathan Edwards: Sermons and Discourses, 1723-1729*, vol. 14, ed. Kenneth P. Minkema, 216-27. New Haven, CT: Yale University Press, 1997.

———. "The Importance of Revival Among Heads of Families." In *Works of Jonathan Edwards: Sermons and Discourses, 1739-1742*, vol. 22, ed. Harry S. Stout and Nathan O. Hatch, with Kyle P. Farley, 451-54. New Haven, CT: Yale University Press, 2003.

———. "In the Name of the Lord of Hosts." In *Works of Jonathan Edwards: Sermons and Discourses, 1743-1758*, vol. 25, ed. Wilson H. Kimnach, 682-84. New Haven, CT: Yale University Press, 2006.

———. Introduction to "Aged Men and Women Joyfully Receiving Christ." In *Works of Jonathan Edwards: Sermons and Discourses, 1739-1742*, vol. 22, ed. Harry S. Stout and Nathan O. Hatch with Kyle P. Farley, 455-57. New Haven, CT: Yale University Press, 2003.

———. Introduction to "Children Ought to Love the Lord Jesus Christ Above All." In *Works of Jonathan Edwards: Sermons and Discourses, 1739-1742*, vol. 22, ed. Harry S. Stout and Nathan O. Hatch, with Kyle P. Farley, 167-69. New Haven, CT: Yale University Press, 2003.

———. Introduction to "Heaven's Dragnet." In *Works of Jonathan Edwards, Sermons and Discourses, 1743-1758*, vol. 25, ed. Wilson H. Kimnach, 575-76. New Haven, CT: Yale University Press, 2006.

———. Introduction to "The Pleasantness of Religion." In *Works of Jonathan Edwards: Sermons and Discourses, 1723-1729*, vol. 14, ed. Kenneth P. Minkema, 97-98. New Haven, CT: Yale University Press, 1997.

———. Introduction to "The Threefold Work of the Holy Ghost." In *Works of Jonathan Edwards: Sermons and Discourses, 1723-1729*, vol. 14, ed. Kenneth P. Minkema, 371-74. New Haven, CT: Yale University Press, 1997.

———. "Justification by Faith Alone." In *Works of Jonathan Edwards: Sermons and Discourses, 1734-1738*, vol. 19, ed. M. X. Lesser, 147-242. New Haven, CT: Yale University Press, 2001.

———. "Like Rain Upon Mown Grass." In *Works of Jonathan Edwards: Sermons and Discourses, 1739-1742*, vol. 22, ed. Harry S. Stout and Nathan O. Hatch with Kyle P. Farley, 300-318. New Haven, CT: Yale University Press, 2003.

———. "None Are Saved by Their Own Righteousness." In *Works of Jonathan Edwards: Sermons and Discourses, 1723-1729*, vol. 14, ed. Kenneth P. Minkema, 332-56. New Haven, CT: Yale University Press, 1992.

_____. "Of Those Who Walk in the Light of God's Countenance." In *Works of Jonathan Edwards: Sermons and Discourses, 1743-1758*, vol. 25, ed. Wilson H. Kimnach, 701-10. New Haven, CT: Yale University Press, 2006.

_____. "Personal Narrative." In *Works of Jonathan Edwards: Letters and Personal Writings, Personal Narrative*, vol. 16, ed. George S. Claghorn, 790-804. New Haven, CT: Yale University Press, 1998.

_____. "Praying for the Spirit." In *Works of Jonathan Edwards: Sermons and Discourses, 1739-1742*, vol. 22, ed. Harry S. Stout and Nathan O. Hatch with Kyle P. Farley, 211-23. New Haven, CT: Yale University Press, 2003.

_____. "The Preciousness of Time." In *Works of Jonathan Edwards: Sermons and Discourses, 1734-1738*, vol. 19, ed. M. X. Lesser, 246-60. New Haven, CT: Yale University Press, 2001.

_____. Preface to "Stupid as Stones." In *Works of Jonathan Edwards: Sermons and Discourses, 1730-1733*, vol. 17, ed. Mark Valeri, 3-44. New Haven, CT: Yale University Press, 1999.

_____. "Pressing into the Kingdom of God." In *Works of Jonathan Edwards: Sermons and Discourses, 1734-1738*, vol. 19, ed. M. X. Lesser, 274-306. New Haven, CT: Yale University Press, 2001.

_____. "Quaestio." In *Works of Jonathan Edwards: Sermons and Discourses, 1723-1729*, vol. 14, ed. Kenneth P. Minkema, 54-66. New Haven, CT: Yale University Press, 1992.

_____. "Qualifications for Full Communion." In *Works of Jonathan Edwards: Sermons and Discourses, 1743-1758*, vol. 25, ed. Wilson H. Kimnach, 353-440. New Haven, CT: Yale University Press, 2006.

_____. "Sacrifice of Christ." In *Works of Jonathan Edwards: Sermons and Discourse, 1723-1729*, vol. 14, ed. Kenneth P. Minkema, 440-57. New Haven, CT: Yale University Press, 1992.

———. "Seeking After Christ." In *Works of Jonathan Edwards: Sermons and Discourses, 1739-1742*, vol. 22, ed. Harry S. Stout and Nathan O. Hatch with Kyle P. Farley, 287-97. New Haven, CT: Yale University Press, 2003.

———. "Sinners in the Hands of an Angry God." In *Works of Jonathan Edwards: Sermons and Discourses, 1739-1742*, vol. 22, ed. Harry S. Stout and Nathan O. Hatch, with Kyle P. Farley, 404-18. New Haven, CT: Yale University Press, 2003.

———. "Sinners in Zion." In *Works of Jonathan Edwards: Sermons and Discourses, 1739-1742*, vol. 22, ed. Harry S. Stout and Nathan O. Hatch with Kyle P. Farley, 265-84. New Haven, CT: Yale University Press, 2003.

———. "Some Thoughts Concerning the Revival." In *Works of Jonathan Edwards: The Great Awakening*, vol. 4, ed. John E. Smith, 289-530. New Haven, CT: Yale University Press, 1972.

———. "Stupid as Stones." In *Works of Jonathan Edwards: Sermons and Discourses, 1730-1733*, vol. 17, ed. Mark Valeri, 175-83. New Haven, CT: Yale University Press, 1999.

———. "The Threefold Work of the Holy Ghost." In *Works of Jonathan Edwards: Sermons and Discourses, 1723-1729*, vol. 14, ed. Kenneth P. Minkema, 375-436. New Haven, CT: Yale University Press, 1997.

———. "True Excellency of a Minister of the Gospel." In *Works of Jonathan Edwards: Sermons and Discourses, 1743-1758*, vol. 25, ed. Wilson H. Kimnach, 84-102. New Haven, CT: Yale University Press, 2006.

———. "True Grace, Distinguished from the Experience of Devils." In *Works of Jonathan Edwards: Sermons and Discourses, 1743-1758*, vol. 25, ed. Wilson H. Kimnach, 608-40. New Haven, CT: Yale University Press, 2006.

———. "Warnings of Future Punishment Don't Seem Real to the Wicked." In *Works of Jonathan Edwards: Sermons and Discourses, 1723-1729*, vol. 14, ed. Kenneth P. Minkema, 200-212. New Haven, CT: Yale University Press, 1997.

———. "Watch and Pray Always (Luke 21:36)." In *Works of Jonathan Edwards: Sermons and Discourses, 1743-1758*, vol. 25, ed. Wilson H. Kimnach, 715-16. New Haven, CT: Yale University Press, 2006.

———. *Works of Jonathan Edwards*, ed. Paul R. Ramsey, vol. 1. New Haven, CT: Yale University Press, 1957. Quoted in Turnbull, Ralph G. *Jonathan Edwards The Preacher*. Grand Rapids: Baker Book House, 1958.

Edwards, Tyron. Introduction to *Charity and Its Fruits: Jonathan Edwards*. Carlisle, PA: Banner of Truth Trust, 1986.

Grosart, Alexander B. *Selections from the Unpublished Writings of Jonathan Edwards*. Ligonier, PA: Soli Deo Gloria Publications, 1992; originally printed by Rev. Alexander B. Grosart for private circulation, 1865.

Gura, Philip F. *Jonathan Edwards, America's Evangelical*. New York: Hill and Wang, A Division of Farrar, Starus, and Giroux, 2005.

Hardman, Keith J. *Seasons of Refreshing, Evangelism and Revivals in America*. Grand Rapids: Baker Book House Co., 1994.

Hart, D. G. *Jonathan Edwards and the Origins of Experimental Calvinism*. Grand Rapids: Baker Academic, 2003.

Hopkins, Samuel. *The Life and Character of the Late Reverend, Learned and Pious Mr. Jonathan Edwards, President of the College of New Jersey, Together With Extracts from His Private Writings and Diary*. 1st ed. Northampton, MA; reprinted by Puritan Reprints, 2007.

———. *Memoirs of Jonathan Edwards (1815)*. Edited by John Hawksley. Kila, MT: Kessinger Publishing, 2009.

———. *The Works of Samuel Hopkins.* Vol. 1. New York: Garland Publishing, 1987.

Jones, Ilion T. *Principles and Practice of Preaching.* Nashville: Abingdon, 1956.

Kimnach, Wilson H. Editor's Comments on "The Gospel Dispensation Is Finished Wholly and Entirely in Free and Glorious Grace." In *Works of Jonathan Edwards: Sermons and Discourses, 1720-1723*, vol. 10, ed. Wilson H. Kimnach, 388-89. New Haven, CT: Jonathan Edwards Center at Yale University, 1992.

———. General Introduction to *The Works of Jonathan Edwards: Sermons and Discourses, 1720-1723*, ed. Wilson H. Kimnach, vol. 10, 3-258. New Haven, CT: Yale University Press, 1992.

———. Introduction to "God's People Should Remember Them that Have Been Their Ministers." In *Works of Jonathan Edwards: Sermons and Discourses, 1743-1758*, vol. 25, ed. Wilson H. Kimnach, 711-12. New Haven, CT: Yale University Press, 2006.

———. Introduction to "In the Name of the Lord of Hosts." In *Works of Jonathan Edwards: Sermons and Discourses, 1743-1758*, vol. 25, ed. Wilson H. Kimnach, 680-81. New Haven, CT: Yale University Press, 2006.

———. Introduction to "Lectures on the Qualifications for Full Communion in the Church of Christ." In *Works of Jonathan Edwards: Sermons and Discourses, 1743-1758*, vol. 25, ed. Wilson H. Kimnach, 349-52. New Haven, CT: Yale University Press, 2006.

———. Introduction to "Literary Milieu." In *The Works of Jonathan Edwards: Sermons and Discourses, 1720-1723*, ed. Wilson H. Kimnach, vol. 10, 3-258. New Haven, CT: Yale University Press, 1992.

———. Introduction to "Saving Faith and Christian Obedience Arise from Godly Love." In *Sermons and Discourses, 1743-1758: The Works of Jonathan Edwards*, vol. 25, ed. Wilson H. Kimnach, 494-96. New Haven, CT: Yale University Press, 2006.

———. Introduction to "A Strong Rod Broken and Withered." In *Works of Jonathan Edwards: Sermons and Discourses, 1743-1758*, ed. Wilson H. Kimnach, vol. 25, 312-14. New Haven, CT: Yale University Press, 2006.

———. Introduction to "Of Those Who Walk in the Light of God's Countenance." In *Works of Jonathan Edwards: Sermons and Discourses, 1743-1758*, vol. 25, ed. Wilson H. Kimnach, 698-700. New Haven, CT: Yale University Press, 2006.

———. Introduction to "True Grace, Distinguished from the Experience of Devils." In *Works of Jonathan Edwards: Sermons and Discourses, 1743-1758*, vol. 25, ed. Wilson H. Kimnach, 605-07. New Haven, CT: Yale University Press, 2006.

———. Preface to "New York Period." In *Works of Jonathan Edwards: Sermons and Discourses, 1720-1723*, vol. 10, ed. Wilson H. Kimnach, 261-93. New Haven, CT: Yale University Press, 1992.

———. Preface to "The Period, 1723-1729." In *Works of Jonathan Edwards: Sermons and Discourses, 1723-1729*, vol. 14, ed. Kenneth P. Minkema, 3-46. New Haven, CT: Yale University Press, 1992.

———. Preface to "The Period, 1743-1758." In *Works of Jonathan Edwards: Sermons and Discourses, 1743-1758*, vol. 25, ed. Wilson H. Kimnach, 3-46. New Haven, CT: Yale University Press, 2006.

———. "The Sermons: Concept and Execution." In *The Princeton Companion to Jonathan Edwards*, ed. Sang Hyun Lee, 250-51. Princeton, NJ: Princeton University Press, 2005.

———. *Works of Jonathan Edwards: Sermons and Discourses, 1720-1723*. Vol. 10. Edited by Wilson H. Kimnach. New Haven, CT: Jonathan Edwards Center at Yale University, 1992.

Goen, C. C. Editor's Introduction to "The Great Awakening: A Faithful Narrative, the Distinguishing Marks, Some Thoughts Concerning the Revival, Letters Relating to the Revival, Preface to True Religion by Joseph Bellamy." In *Works of Jonathan Edwards: The Great Awakening*, vol. 4, ed. John E. Smith, 1-95. New Haven, CT: Yale University Press, 1972.

Kimnach, Wilson H. "Preface to the Period." In *Works of Jonathan Edwards: Sermons and Discourses, 1743-1758*, vol. 25, ed. Wilson H. Kimnach, 3-46. New Haven, CT: Yale University Press, 2006.

Kroll, Woodrow Michael. *Prescription for Preaching*. Grand Rapids: Baker Publishing Group, 1980.

Lawson, Steven J. *The Unwavering Resolve of Jonathan Edwards*. Orlando: Reformation Trust Publishing, 2008.

Lee, Sang Hyun, ed. *The Princeton Companion to Jonathan Edwards*. Princeton: Princeton University Press, 2005.

Lee, Sang Hyun, and Allen C. Guelzo, eds. *Edwards in Our Time*. Grand Rapids: William B. Eerdmans Publishing Co., 1999.

Lesser, M. X. Appendix B. "Dated Sermons, January 1734-December 1738." In *Works of Jonathan Edwards: Sermons and Discourses, 1734-1738*, vol. 19, ed. M. X. Lesser, 801. New Haven, CT: Yale University Press, 2001.

_____. Introduction to "Pressing into the Kingdom of God." In *Works of Jonathan Edwards: Sermons and Discourses, 1734-1738*, vol. 19, ed. M. X. Lesser, 272-73. New Haven, CT: Yale University Press, 2001.

_____. *Jonathan Edwards: A Reference Guide*. Boston: G. K. Hall, 1981.

_____. Preface to "The Period." In *Works of Jonathan Edwards: Sermons and Discourses, 1734-1738*, vol. 19, ed. M. X. Lesser, 3-36. New Haven, CT: Yale University Press, 2001.

Levesque, George G. Introduction to "Quaestio." In *Works of Jonathan Edwards: Sermons and Discourses, 1723-1729*, vol. 14, ed. Kenneth P. Minkema, 47-53. New Haven, CT: Yale University Press, 1992.

MacArthur, John. *Twelve Ordinary Men, How the Master Shaped His Disciples for Greatness, and What He Wants to Do with You.* Nashville: W Publishing Group, A Division of Thomas Nelson, 2002.

Marsden, George M. *Jonathan Edwards: A Life*. New Haven, CT: Yale University Press, 2003.

Marshall, Peter, and David Manuel. *The Light and the Glory*. Old Tappan, NJ: Fleming H. Revell Co., 1977.

Maxwell, John C. *Winning with People*. Nashville: Thomas Nelson Publishers, 2004.

May, Henry F. "Jonathan Edwards and America." In *Jonathan Edwards and the American Experience*, ed. Nathan O. Hatch and Harry S. Stout, 19-33. New York: Oxford University Press, 1988.

McClymond, Michael J. *Encounters with God: An Approach to the Theology of Jonathan Edwards*. New York: Oxford University Press, 1998.

McDermott, Gerald R. *Jonathan Edwards Confronts the Gods*. New York: Oxford University Press, 2000.

Miller, Perry. *Jonathan Edwards*. Toronto: George J. McLeod & William Sloan Associates, 1949.

_____., ed. *Images or Shadows of Divine Things by Jonathan Edwards*. New Haven, CT: Yale University Press, 1949.

Moody, Josh. *Jonathan Edwards and the Enlightenment: Knowing the Presence of God*. Lanham, MD: University Press of America, 1992.

Murray, Iain H. *Jonathan Edwards: A New Biography*. Carlisle, PA: Banner of Truth Trust, 1992.

Nichols, Stephen J. "Last of the Mohican Missionaries, Jonathan Edwards at Stockbridge." In *American Religion and the Evangelical Tradition: The Legacy of Jonathan Edwards*, ed. D. G. Hart, Sean Michael Lucas, and Stephen J. Nichols, 47-63. Grand Rapids: Baker Book House, 2003.

Pearcey, Nancy. *Total Truth, Liberating Christianity from Its Cultural Captivity*. Wheaton, IL: Crossway Books, 2005.

Prince, Thomas, John Webb, Thomas Foxcroft, and Mather Byles. Preface to "An Humble Inquiry into the Rules of the Word of God Concerning the Qualifications Requisite to a Complete Standing and Full Communion in the Visible Christian Church." In *Works of Jonathan Edwards: Ecclesiastical Writings*, vol. 12, ed. David D. Hall, 172-73. New Haven, CT: Yale University Press, 1994.

Rainer Thom S., and Eric Geiger. *Simple Church*. Nashville: Broadman & Holman Publishers, 2006.

Ramsey, Paul R. Editor's Introduction to "Freedom of the Will." In *Works of Jonathan Edwards*, vol. 1, ed. Paul R. Ramsey, 1-128. New Haven, CT: Yale University Press, 1957.

Robinson, Haddon W. *Biblical Preaching: The Development and Delivery of Expository Messages*. Grand Rapids: Baker Book House, 1994.

Schafer, Thomas A. Appendix: Dated Batches of Sermons, 1730-1732, and Dated Sermons, January-December 1733. In *Works of Jonathan Edwards: Sermons and Discourses, 1730-1733*, vol. 17, ed. Mark Valeri, 447-58. New Haven, CT: Yale University Press, 1999.

_____. Editor's Introduction to *The Works of Jonathan Edwards: The "Miscellanies,"* vol. 13, 1-90. New Haven, CT: Yale University Press, 1994.

Smith, John E. *Jonathan Edwards: Puritan, Preacher, Philosopher*. Notre Dame, IN: University of Notre Dame Press, 1992.

Smith, Steven W. *Dying to Preach: Embracing the CROSS in the PULPIT*. Grand Rapids: Kregel Academic and Professional, 2009.

Sproul, R. C. *Chosen by God*. Wheaton, IL: Tyndale House Publishers, 1986.

Stein, Stephen J. Editor's Introduction. "The Blank Bible." In *Works of Jonathan Edwards*, vol. 24, Part I, ed. Wilson H. Kimnach, 1-117. New Haven, CT: Jonathan Edwards Center at Yale University, 2006. Quoting Edwards, Jonathan. "Personal Narrative." In *Works of Jonathan Edwards: Letters and Personal Writings, Personal Narrative*, ed. George S. Claghorn, 790-804. New Haven, CT: Yale University Press, 1998), 16:797.

_____. Editor's Introduction. "The Blank Bible." In *Works of Jonathan Edwards*, vol. 24, Part I, ed. Wilson H. Kimnach, 1-117. New Haven, CT: Jonathan Edwards Center at Yale University, 2006. Quoting Edwards, Jonathan. "Resolutions." In *Works of Jonathan Edwards, Letters and Personal Writings, Resolutions*, vol. 16, ed. George S. Claghorn, 753-59. New Haven, CT: Yale University Press, 1998.

Stiles, Ezra. "May 24, 1779 Entry." In *The Literary Diary of Ezra Stiles*, vol. 2, ed. Franklin B. Dexter, 337. New York: Scribner's, 1901.

Stoddard, Samuel. *A Plea for Fervent Preaching: The Defects of Preachers Reproved*. Boston: n.p., 1724.

Stott, John R. W. *Between Two Worlds: The Art of Preaching in the Twentieth Century*. Grand Rapids: William B. Eerdmans Publishing Co., 1982.

Stoughton, John A. *Windsor Farmes: A Glimpse of an Old Parish*. Hartford, CT: n.p., 1883.

Stout, Harry S. Editor's Introduction to "The Importance of Revival Among Heads of Families." In *Works of Jonathan Edwards: Sermons and Discourses, 1739-1742*, vol. 22, ed. Harry S. Stout and Nathan O. Hatch with Kyle P. Farley, 448-50. New Haven, CT: Yale University Press, 2003.

_____. *The New England Soul: Preaching and Religious Culture in Colonial New England*. New York: Oxford University Press, 1986.

———. "The Puritans and Edwards." In the *Princeton Companion to Jonathan Edwards*, ed. Sang Hyun Lee, 250-52. Princeton, NJ: Princeton University Press, 2005.

Sweeney Douglas A. "An Essay in American Religion and the Evangelical Tradition: The Legacy of Jonathan Edwards." *Taylorites, Tylerites, and the Dissolution of the New England Theology*, ed. D. G. Hart, Sean Michael Lucas, and Stephen J. Nichols, 181-99. Grand Rapids: Baker Academic, 2003.

Thuesen, Peter J. *Works of Jonathan Edwards, Catalogues of Books, Note to the Reader*. New Haven, CT: Yale University Press, 2008.

Tracy, Joseph. *The Great Awakening: A History of the Revival of Religion in the Time of Edwards and Whitefield*. Boston: Tappan and Dennet, 1842.

Tracy, Patricia J. *Jonathan Edwards Pastor: Religion and Society in Eighteenth Century Northampton*. New York, Hill and Wang, 1979.

Trumbull, James R. *History of Northampton, Massachusetts from Its Settlement in 1654*. Northampton: Gazette Printing, 1902.

Turnbull, Ralph G. *Jonathan Edwards the Preacher*. Grand Rapids: Baker Book House, 1958.

Valeri, Mark, ed. Editor's Introduction to "God Glorified in Man's Dependence." In *Works of Jonathan Edwards: Sermons and Discourses, 1730-1733*, vol. 17, 196-99. New Haven, CT: Yale University Press, 1999.

Vines, Jerry, and Jim Shaddix. *Power in the Pulpit: How to Prepare and Deliver Expository Sermons*. Chicago: Moody Press, 1999.

Von Rohr, John. *The Shaping of American Congregationalism 162-1957*. Cleveland, OH: Pilgrim Press, 1992.

Winslow, Ola. *Jonathan Edwards 1703-1758*. New York: Collier Publishing Co., 1961.

## Articles

Aldridge, Marion. "George Whitefield: The Necessary Interdependence of Preaching Style and Sermon Content to Effect Revival." *Journal of the Evangelical Theological Society* 23, no. 1 (March 1980): 55-64.

Ehrhard, Jim. "A Critical Analysis of the Tradition of Jonathan Edwards as a Manuscript Preacher." *Westminster Journal of Theology* 60 (1988): 73-76.

Hannah, John D. "Jonathan Edwards and the Art of Effective Communication." *Reformation & Revival* 11, no. 4 (Fall 2002): 109-31.

Holbrook, Clyde A. "Jonathan Edwards and His Detractors." *Theology Today* 10, no. 3 (October 1953): 384-96.

Logan, Samuel T. "The Hermeneutics of Jonathan Edwards." *Westminster Theological Journal* 43 (1980): 79-96.

Miller, Perry. "Old Age in the Religion in the Writings and Life of Jonathan Edwards." *Church History* 70, no. 4 (December 2001): 674-704.

Nichols, Stephen J. "The Mind Shapers." *Christian History* 77 (2003): 20-22.

Rivera, T. "Jonathan Edwards's 'Hermeneutic': A Case Study of the Sermon, 'Christian Knowledge'." *Journal of the Evangelical Theological Society* 49, no. 2 (June 2006): 273-86.

Turnbull, Ralph G. "Jonathan Edwards: A Voice for God." *Christianity Today*, January 6, 1958, 9.

Winiarski, Douglas L. "Jonathan Edwards, Enthusiast?: Radical Revivalism and the Great Awakening in the Connecticut Valley." *Church History* 74, no. 4 (December 2005): 683-739.

## Ph.D. Dissertations

Holloway, Charles Stewart. "The Homiletical Theology of Jonathan Edwards, Gilbert Tennant, and Samuel Davies." Ph.D. diss., Southwestern Baptist Theological Seminary, 2008.

Wheeler, Rachel M. "Living Upon Hope: Mohicans and Missionaries, 1730-1760." Ph.D. diss., Yale University, 1999.

## Electronic Sources

Barna Group. "A Profile of Protestant Pastors in Anticipation of 'Pastor Appreciation Month'" [on-line]. Accessed February 12, 2012; available at http://www.barna.org/ barna-update/article/5-barna-update/59-a-profile-of-protestant-pastors-in-anticipation-of-qpastor-appreciation-monthq?q=years+service; Internet.

Burr, Esther. "February 14, 1747 Entry." *Journal of Esther Burr*, ed. Jeremiah Eames Ranking, 33 [on-line]. Accessed December 28, 2009; available at Books.google. com; Internet.

_____. "September 14, 1743 Entry." *Journal of Esther Burr*, ed. Jeremiah Eames Ranking, 26 [on-line]. Accessed December 28, 2009; available at Books.google. com; Internet.

_____. "1751 Entry." *Journal of Esther Burr*, ed. Jeremiah Eames Ranking, 25-47 [on-line]. Accessed December 28, 2009; available at Books.google.com; Internet.

_____. "January 1754 Entry." *Journal of Esther Burr*, ed. Jeremiah Eames Ranking, 79 [on-line]. Accessed December 28, 2009; available at Books.google.com; Internet.

_____. "September 2, 1757 Entry." *Journal of Esther Burr*, ed. Jeremiah Eames Ranking, 93 [on-line]. Accessed December 28, 2009; available at Books.google. com; Internet.

Car Insurance Comparison. "Clergy/Pastor/Bishop/Priest Car Insurance Rates" [on-line]. Accessed February 2, 2012; available at http://www.carinsurancecomparison.com/ clergypastorbishoppriest-car-insurance-rates/; Internet.

Edwards, Jonathan. "Heaven and Earth Shall Pass Away, but My Word Shall Not Pass Away." *Sermons*. Series II. *WJE Online* 42 (1743). Jonathan Edwards Center at Yale University [on-line]. Accessed 16 December 2009; available at http://edwards.yale. edu; Internet.

_____. "Ministers to Preach Not Their Own Wisdom but the Word of God." *Sermons*. Series II. *WJE Online* 55 (January-June 1740). Jonathan Edwards Center at Yale University [on-line]. Accessed 16 December 2009; available at http://edwards. yale.edu; Internet.

_____. "Ordain Elders in Every Church, Acts 14:23." Ordination Sermon for Chester Williams at Hadley." *Sermons*. Series II. *WJE Online* 57 (January-June 1741). Jonathan Edwards Center at Yale University [on-line]. Accessed 16 December 2009; available at http://edwards.yale.edu; Internet.

_____. "Thy Name Is as Ointment Poured Forth." *Sermons*. Series II. *WJE Online* 48 (1733): 1. Jonathan Edwards Center at Yale University [on-line]. Accessed 16 December 2009; available at http://edwards.yale.edu; Internet.

Minkema, Kenneth P. *A Chronology of Edwards' Life and Writings*. New Haven, CT: Jonathan Edwards Center At Yale University, 1-4 [on-line]. Accessed 18 December 2009; available at http://edwards.yale.edu/research/chronology; Internet.

National Park Service. U.S. Department of the Interior. "Gideon Clark," 1 [on-line]. Accessed 16 December 2009; available at www.nps.gov/spar/historyculture/upload/ Gideon_Clark_bio.doc; Internet.

Sherman, Daniel, "Pastor Burnout Statistics" [on-line]. Accessed February 12, 2012; available at http://www.pastorburnout.com/pastor-burnout-statistics.html; Internet.

"Solomon Stoddard" (March 2007) [on-line]. Accessed 28 December 2009; available at http://wikipedia.org/wiki/Solomon-Stoddard; Internet.

*Wikipedia Online.* S.v. "S. Parkes Cadman" [on-line]. Accessed February 2, 2012; available at http://en.wikipedia.org/wiki/Televangelism; Internet.

_____. S.v. "Steve Jobs and Apple Computer" [on-line]. Accessed February 2, 2012; available at http://en.wikipedia.org/wiki/Steve_Jobs; Internet.

_____. S.v. "Who was the First Radio Preacher?" [on-line]. Accessed February 2, 2012; available at http://en.wikipedia.org/wiki/Televangelism; Internet.

### Personal Letters, Sermons, and Miscellaneous

Edwards, Jonathan. "God Is Himself the Fire that Shall Destroy and Consume Wicked Men (Heb. 12:29)." Jonathan Edwards Collection, MSS 151, Box 14, Folder 1128. New Haven, CT: Yale University, Beinecke Library, May 1742.

_____. "God's People Should Remember Them that Have Been Their Minister (Heb 13:7-8)." Jonathan Edwards Collection, MSS 151, Box 14, Folder 1128. New Haven, CT: Yale University, Beinecke Library, May 1742.

_____. "A Good Man Is A Happy Man, Whatever His Outward Condition Is, Isaiah 3:10." *Writings of Jonathan Edwards*, Gen MSS 151, Box 13, Folder 994. New Haven, CT: Yale University, Beinecke Library Rare Books and Manuscripts, 1720's Sermons.

_____. "Impending Judgments Averted Only By Reformation (Jonah 3:10)." Jonathan Edwards Collection, MSS 151, Box 13, Folder 1012. New Haven, CT: Yale University, Beinecke Library, May 1742.

———. "Letter to the Trustees of the College of New Jersey." In *Works of Jonathan Edwards: Letters and Personal Writings, Personal Narrative*, vol. 16, ed. George S. Claghorn, 725-30. New Haven, CT: Yale University Press, 1998.

———. "My Farewell Sermon to the People of Northampton (II Cor. 1:14)." Jonathan Edwards Collection, MSS 151, Box 14, Folder 1107. New Haven, CT: Yale University, Beinecke Library, July 1, 1750.

———. Personal letter to Benjamin Coleman. In *Works of Jonathan Edwards: Letters and Personal Writings, Personal Narrative*, vol. 16, ed. George S. Claghorn, 48-49. New Haven, CT: Yale University Press, 1998.

———. Personal letter to Deacon Moses Lyman, 10 May 1742. In *Works of Jonathan Edwards: Letters and Personal Writings, Personal Narrative*, vol. 16, ed. George S. Claghorn, 101-02. New Haven, CT: Yale University Press, 1998.

———. Personal letter to Joseph Hawley Jr., 18 November 1754. In Jonathan Edwards, *Works of Jonathan Edwards: Letters and Personal Writings, Personal Narrative*, ed. George S. Claghorn, vol. 16, 646-55. New Haven, CT: Yale University Press, 1998.

———. Personal letter to Rev. John Erskine, 5 July 1750. In *Works of Jonathan Edwards: Letters and Personal Writings, Personal Narrative*, vol. 16, ed. George S. Claghorn, 347-56. New Haven, CT: Yale University Press, 1998.

———. Personal letter to The Reverend Thomas Foxcroft, 24 May 1749. In Jonathan Edwards, *Works of Jonathan Edwards: Letters and Personal Writings, Personal Narrative*, vol. 16, ed. George S. Claghorn, 282-86. New Haven, CT: Yale University Press, 1998.

———. Personal letter to The Reverend Thomas Foxcroft, 11 February 1757. In Jonathan Edwards, *Works of Jonathan Edwards: Letters and Personal Writings, Personal Narrative*, vol. 16, ed. George S. Claghorn, 695-97. New Haven, CT: Yale University Press, 1998.

———. Personal letter to Rev. William McCulloch, 11 February 1757. In *Works of Jonathan Edwards: Letters and Personal Writings, Personal Narrative*, vol. 16, ed. George S. Claghorn, 684-87. New Haven, CT: Yale University Press, 1998.

———. Personal letter to Timothy Edwards, January 1752. In *Works of Jonathan Edwards: Letters and Personal Writings, Personal Narrative*, vol. 16, ed. George S. Claghorn, 420-21. New Haven, CT: Yale University Press, 1998.

———. "What I Intend at this Time to Shew [Is] What We Are Taught Concerning Christ by These Names by Which He Is . . . Called (Rev. 1:5(a)." Edwards Collection, MSS 151, Box 14, Folder 1139. New Haven, CT: Yale University, Beinecke Library, June 1745.

Edwards, Timothy. A June 13, 1742 Sermon on Ecclesiastes 9:10. New Haven, CT: Beinecke Library, Box 24, Folder 1371.

———. A July 25, 1742 Sermon on Job 14:5. New Haven, CT: Beinecke Library, Box 24, Folder 1371.

———. A December 1705 sermon on Isaiah 55:7. New Haven, CT: Beinecke Library, Box 24, Folder 1366.

———. A December 1705 Sermon on Jeremiah 4:18. New Haven, CT: Beinecke Library, Box 24, Folder 1367.

———. A 1740s Sermon on John 15:6. New Haven, CT: Beinecke Library, Box 24, Folder 1365.

Pelton, Helen. *Timothy Edwards (1669-1758)*. South Windsor, CT Library Board, a booklet published by South Windsor Historical Society, information compiled by staff of Wood Memorial Library, Spring 1968.

Stoddard, Solomon. "A Plea for Fervent Preaching: The Defects of Preachers Reproved." Sermon preached at Northampton, May 19, 1723. Boston: n.p., 1724.

Twain, Mark. "Letter to Rev. Joseph H. Twitchell" (February 1902). In *Mark Twain's Letters*, ed. Albert Bigelow Paine, vol. 2, 719-21. New York: Harper, 1917.

## Paper Presented ETS Regional Meeting

Easley, Toby. "Jonathan Edwards: Extemporaneous or Manuscript Preacher?" Academic paper presented at the ETS Regional Meeting, March 23-24, 2007, Southwestern Baptist Theological Seminary, Fort Worth, Texas.

# NEW ENGLAND PHOTOS

170  JONATHAN EDWARDS: BEYOND THE MANUSCRIPTS

The graves of Jonathan Edwards's parents in East Windsor, Connecticut.

Yale University

First Congregational Church, Hadley, Massachusetts.

"The Manse," Solomon Stoddard's home in Northampton, Massachusetts.

The gates to the East Windsor, Connecticut cemetery.

Historical stone marking the Church at Enfield, where Edwards preached his famous "Sinners" sermon.

The Stockbridge Mission House built by John Sergeant in 1742.

## BIRTHPLACE OF JONATHAN EDWARDS

First American theologian and philosopher. Born in 1703, son of Timothy Edwards. He graduated from Yale at age 17, was pastor in Bolton, tutor at Yale, missionary at Stockbridge, and in 1758 became pres. of Princeton University where he died. His grandson, Aaron Burr, became 3rd vice-president of U. S.

The sign marking the birthplace of Jonathan Edwards, East Windsor, Connecticut.

Historic red house on the street near Edwards place of birth in East Windsor, Connecticut.

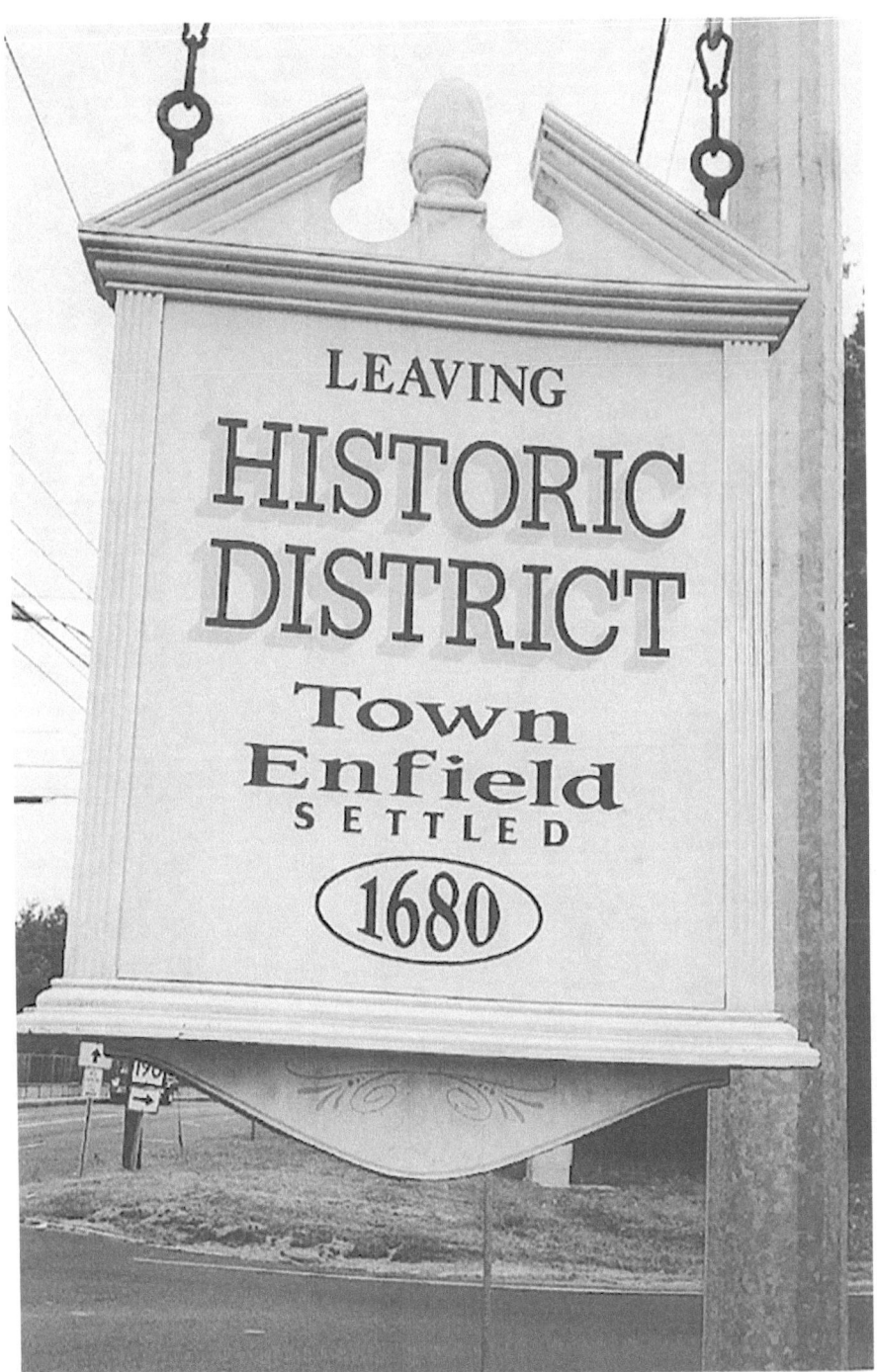

Historic sign located at the north end of Enfield, Connecticut.

The Site marking the Edwards house in Stockbridge, Massachusetts.

The Congregational Church in Stockbridge, Massachusetts.

The "Sinners" sermon outline (1741).

Courtesy of Jonathan Edwards Collection, Yale University Library Beinecke Rare Book and Manuscript Library.

Jonathan Edwards (1703-1758)  Sarah Edwards (1710-1758)

www.ingramcontent.com/pod-product-compliance
Lightning Source LLC
Chambersburg PA
CBHW021126300426
44113CB00006B/309